Entry into Life

Entry into Life

The Gospel of Death

GEORGE APPLETON

formerly Anglican Archbishop in Jerusalem

Darton, Longman and Todd
London

First published 1985 by
Darton, Longman & Todd Ltd
89 Lillie Road, London SW6 1UD

© 1985 George Appleton

ISBN 0 232 51600 6

British Library Cataloguing in Publication Data

Appleton, George
  Entry into life: the gospel of death.
  1. Death—Religious aspects—Christianity
  I. Title
248.4   BT825

ISBN 0–232–51600–6

Phototypeset by Input Typesetting Ltd., London SW19 8DR
Printed and bound in Great Britain by
Anchor Brendon Ltd
Tiptree Essex

IN

GRATEFUL REMEMBRANCE

OF

HELEN GOLD

a comfort to many people
in bereavement, who had
hoped to be a partner in
writing this book.
She became a risen one
on 6 December 1982,
a courageous and loving soul.

Contents

Acknowledgments

Unless otherwise stated, the Scripture quotations in this publication are from the Revised Standard Version of the Bible, copyrighted 1971 and 1952 by the division of Christian Education of the National Council of the Churches of Christ in the USA. Extracts from the Book of Common Prayer 1662, which is Crown Copyright in the United Kingdom, are reproduced by permission of Eyre & Spottiswoode, Her Majesty's Printers London. Thanks are due to S.P.C.K. for permission to quote from *My God My Glory* by Eric Milner-White.

I am most grateful to the husband of Helen Gold for allowing me to quote from her letter to me (pp. 78–9) and to another friend of mine for allowing me to quote from his letter to me (pp. 81–2).

Three of my own prayers (on pp. 42 and 111–12) were previously published in my *Prayers for a Troubled Heart* (Darton, Longman and Todd 1983).

My debt to certain writers for insights and inspiration is gratefully acknowledged in footnotes, as also to the publishers of the books from which quotation is made.

G.A.

Introduction

A number of reasons prompted the writing of this small book. The first is that in age I am now approaching the frontier between this world and the next, and must shortly cross it. So I am interested in learning all I can about it. The second arises out of pastoral contacts with the dying and gratitude to them for confiding in me their hopes and fears.

A third reason is a hope to comfort those in bereavement and loss, not only for the death of their loved ones but in the months and years of loneliness that follow. I now do this with empathy, for I stand in shoes similar to theirs and speak from experience.

I am deeply grateful to a number of writers who have not only given me new insights, but have sometimes confirmed impulses of faith rising within my own spirit which I had not previously dared to express. Some of these are named in the text, and their books mentioned in footnotes.

Personal contacts with people of other faith to my own have shown what a widespread interest there is in the fact and meaning of death. Their experience, their thoughts, fears, hopes and findings have convinced me of a spiritual kinship, and also that there is something in Christianity and other religions which is of common origin, Someone or Something eternally transcendent and universally immanent. This is so whether those contacts are with contemporary living people, as those among whom I lived and travelled in my early years in Burma, or from a growing study of their scriptures and traditions, for example the Egyptian and Tibetan Books of the Dead, which we Christians have not yet studied in depth.

I hope that the pages which follow will show the depth of my own discipleship to Jesus of Nazareth both in the days of Galilee and Jerusalem, and in the eternal years of his Risen Life.

July 1984   + George Appleton

1

Becoming Acquainted with Death

My earliest memory of death goes back to when I was six or seven years of age when our much loved terrier dog Towser died. He had become ill, refused to eat and looked with sad eyes as my father, mother and a younger brother or I stroked him and tempted him to eat. Vets were few and far between, but country people had a knowledge born of working with animals. Several neighbours were called in and sadly suggested that Towser should be put out of his misery. We all wept and for days afterwards were sad. Towser's body was buried in a corner of the garden and flowers were planted on his grave, wild flowers gathered from the village lanes. This first experience of death was tearfully sad. The second was different.

I went to the village school. The headmistress with her only assistant, who happened to be her sister, did not want to live in the schoolhouse, so it was occupied by an old lady and her daughter and son-in-law. Every day as we schoolchildren went home for dinner she would stand at her door and smilingly greet us, and I somehow got into the habit of going in to see her, wet or fine. Then one day she fell ill, but I was still invited in, and saw her in bed, which was placed near the window so that she could look out on to the path leading through the garden to the school. A few days later her daughter told me with tears that she had died. I still went in, and there she was, seemingly asleep on her bed. I stroked her face and was surprised to find it cold and unanswering, and was told that she was gone to be with Jesus. Day school, Sunday school, church and home and a birthday picture book had given me the imagination of Jesus as a very kind and loving person, and I knew that Granny Biddiscomb was all right if she was with him.

My father was gardener to the village squire and the house in which we lived was next to the churchyard. In our small village the number of funerals were few, but whenever there was one I as a small boy of eight or nine would help the sexton dig the grave and fill it in afterwards. I never had the feeling that the person who had died was in the coffin but that he had gone to be with Jesus.

When I was ten years old the family left Somerset and went to live in Maidenhead. Two years later the First World War broke out and my father enlisted before conscription was brought in. He served in France, mostly as a guard on troop trains or ammunition trains. Every day in the newspapers there were whole pages of the casualties sustained. I remember one dreadful weekend when a hundred thousand British men had died in an attack. There was always a fear in our minds that a telegram would be delivered announcing my father's death or that his name might appear in the endless lists of daily casualties. In our parish church where I was a choirboy there was a special service of intercession every Friday night when the names of all the men at the front from our parish would be remembered and also those of the men who had died. My father survived the war, but never a talkative man he did not tell us much about his experiences in France. Then came the war memorials in every church or village and the annual service on armistice day, of thanksgiving for victory and in remembrance of the fallen.

In my first curacy at Stepney in a parish of forty thousand, funerals were frequent and it was not thought appropriate to bury the body until it had been kept for at least a week, and I well remember the smell of death as I tried to organize prayers for the dead and also those of comfort for the many hopelessly mourning. On one occasion I was sent by my rector to do duty at the big Bow cemetery, as the regular chaplain was ill. It was well known to the local clergy that he was an alcoholic. The feeling aroused in my mind was not so much a criticism of him, but of puzzled dismay that the ecclesiastical and cemetery authorities seemed to rate the ministry to mourners at such a low priority. On that particular day I officiated at fourteen interments, five to each grave, and met groups of mourners with whom I had had no previous contact. It took me days to recover from that experience and from the sight of mourners, whom I had not yet the spiritual maturity nor the pastoral technique to comfort with the assurance of the continuing life, and a better kind of life, of God's loving providence.

From Stepney I went to Burma as a missionary and was impressed by two new experiences: the quietness and trust at most Christian funerals; and the way in which the cremation of a Buddhist monk was always an occasion of festivity, the assumption being that the holy man had at last attained to Nirvana, the sphere of ineffable bliss. My later years in Burma were during the Second World War when Rangoon was frequently bombed after the entry of Japan into the war. The bombs were aimed at personnel rather than the destruction of buildings, and I remember often going into the city after a raid and seeing corpses lying in the streets. Finally came the dropping of the first atomic bomb on Hiroshima with the news that sixty thousand people had died in a flash. Later we learned of the dreadful radiation when a further sixty thousand people died and many others suffered from its long term effects.

Even before that widespread destruction I had learnt of the even greater death-roll in Hitler's attempt to destroy the Jews of Europe, when six million Jews and perhaps nearly as many gentiles in Eastern Europe were liquidated in the gas chambers.

Soon after the ending of the Second World War I returned to England and as part of my pastoral responsibility in a City of London church I became part-time chaplain of the Hospital for Sick Children in Great Ormond Street, to which children from all over the world are brought by their parents in the hope of cure. There I would often be called, late at night or at any time during the day, to baptise dying babies. I can still remember very vividly holding such little ones in my arms and, with only a compassionate nurse to represent the Church, admitting them into the family of Christ, hoping that my pastoral ministration and the care of the hospital staff could somehow witness to the loving compassion of God and the Church's faith that these small scraps of humanity were safe in his care.

There was, however, one moving and inspiring development during my three years part-time ministry at Great Ormond Street. The matron, Miss Gwen Kirby, and I were eager to make the little mortuary chapel where relatives came to view the little corpses of their children a place of faith and comfort. Together we called to our aid Josephine das Vasconsellos, a sculptress whose work included the planning of Christmas cribs and other religious statuary. She modelled a representation of the hands of God coming down from the top of a memorial board and the little hands of a child coming up with a flower in them, and underneath, the text which had been in the little chapel before, going back to the prophet Elisha and a farmer's wife in biblical Israel; a text which in the situation of the Hospital for Sick Children gained a new relevance: 'Is it well with the child? It is well.'

Over twenty years later, after service in Western Australia and Jerusalem, my wife had a stroke, the result of which was that she could neither talk or walk. Our doctor warned us that she would almost certainly die, but to his astonishment and to our thankfulness she lived for five years after the stroke, during which time my family and I were able to show her our thankfulness and love. Gradually her condition worsened and to get the necessary nursing care I rented a flat in St Luke's Nursing Home, Oxford and also acted as honorary chaplain to the other residents. During the time we were there I was involved in some way or other with the death of forty-two people, which ultimately included my wife. It was in that personal and pastoral experience that my own faith was tested and my own search for a deeper understanding of ageing, dying, death and bereavement was undertaken.

2

Death a Fact of Life

For many generations there has been a reluctance to talk about death, which has been described as man's last taboo. Our generation is different, for we have witnessed death on a scale that no earlier generation has known. The twentieth century, which still has several years to run, has seen two world wars and a hundred or more local wars, in which a hundred million people have died. There is the fact of nuclear energy and its effect on genetic heritage as seen at Hiroshima; more and more people die of cancer which seems to be a nuclear multiplication of lethal cells; in war civil populations are bombed indiscriminately and there is a frightening fall in the valuation of human life. Terrorists seem able to inflict death as compulsive blackmail and professional murderers to kill named individuals; in undernourished nations hundreds of thousands die from starvation and it is said that every day forty thousand children perish before they have had a chance to live.

Every family, sooner or later, is stricken by the death of someone they love: widows and widowers who for many years enjoyed a deep loving relationship find themselves bereaved and lonely;

parents are heartbroken by the premature death of a beloved child. We cannot avoid the fact and problem of death. There is the smell and fear of death everywhere.

For religious people death raises the question of the goodness of God. It is my purpose to face the question frankly and honestly. I know that I cannot prove by logic or scientific examination that there is life after death; all I can do is to examine my own experience, to think and hope, and to express the conviction and faith summed up in the closing words of the Christian creed: 'And I look for the resurrection of the dead and the life of the world to come.' More than that, I must determine to think and live in that faith: I must choose to believe in God, eternal life and unfailing love.

In that wrestling for faith there are things that I can and must believe and there are certain things that I cannot and do not believe. The greatest revelation of the Bible to me is the conviction that 'God is love' (1 John 4:16). God was in Christ showing us in terms of a human life his nature, character and will, reconciling men to God (2 Corinthians 5:19–20), and it is his purpose and will that all people shall come to the truth and be saved for eternal life and blessedness (1 Timothy 2:3–4). There are also things in the Bible that seem more like the thinking of humans, that represent a stage in religious experience and formulation, rather than a word of God, interim assumptions that later had to be corrected and perfected, and sometimes abandoned.

One assumption, accepted by the writer of the

Book of Genesis, is that physical death is the punishment of the sin of a mythical Eve and Adam, rather than God's providential ordering of human life. But if God is love it must be good, more of a new beginning than an end, not less life but more life, a birth from the womb of the physical, material, mortal, perishable, into a final birth into the spiritual, the eternal, the imperishable, the immortal, the new order which God has planned and offers to all who love him and also to those who do not yet do so. One of the almost unbelievable biblical insights to me is that God can hold in his consciousness, concern and love not only the four thousand million at present living, but all who have died in the past and the potentially greater number still to be born. I often wonder if there is a parallel in the micro-chip: might we not think of God as the original and personal micro-chip, with n^n relationships of love simultaneously held in the divine heart.

I am completely satisfied and even happy to believe that sin ultimately kills all spiritual life, though I am equally convinced of the patience of God, who like Jesus seeks for every lost sheep until he finds it. At the same time I recognize that each of us has free will and can refuse to be found and saved.

One of the earliest Jewish Christian writers believes that the fear of death is our real trouble and says that 'Jesus himself partook of the same nature [*as ourselves*], that through death he might destroy him who has the power of death, that is the devil, and deliver all those who through fear of death were subject to lifelong bondage' (Hebrews

2:14–15). Jesus said, 'Do not fear those that kill the body but cannot kill the soul; rather fear him who can destroy both soul and body in hell' (Matthew 10:28). I interpret this to mean that the devil can kill the soul as well as the body, if we allow him to do so.

At death the spirit (the real and essential self) leaves the body, which is no longer the willing and able instrument of the spirit that it once was. St Paul warns us that flesh and blood cannot inherit the kingdom of God but he also insists that in God's new order of being each of us will be given a spiritual body. This suggests to me that the body may be thought of as something different from flesh and blood, it is rather the entity that gives life and form.

I also dare to doubt the common assumption that the date of our death is already determined by God. I rather believe that we die from natural causes or from accident or by the malice or callous indifference of men.

Yet having expressed this doubt I have learnt from pastoral and personal experience of dying people that many do get an intuitional feeling that death is near, that they need to put their affairs in order, that the time of physical sight and touch of their loved ones will cease in the near future; and in the initial realization of this warning there is a sadness which needs to be recognized, accepted and if possible welcomed.

A proper preface in the eucharistic prayers of the Alternative Service Book of the Anglican Church sums up this difficult chapter comfortingly and convincingly: 'although death comes to us all, yet we rejoice in the promise of eternal life; for to your faithful people life is changed, not taken away; and when our mortal flesh is laid aside, an everlasting dwelling place is made ready for us in heaven'.

3

A Process of Transition

Death is an event, something that will happen to all of us. Ageing will be experienced by many of us. Dying may be sudden or may be a short period or long drawn out. Whatever may be the case it is a process of transition, from this world to the next, from mortality to immortality. It should therefore be a time of preparation, not only of reluctant acceptance, but of joyful expectation.

St Paul concludes his great chapter on resurrection with these words:

> Lo! I tell you a mystery. We shall not all sleep, but we shall all be changed, in a moment, in the twinkling of an eye, at the last trumpet. For the trumpet will sound, and the dead will be raised imperishable, and we shall be changed. For this perishable nature must put on the imperishable, and this mortal nature must put on immortality. When the perishable puts on the imperishable, and the mortal puts on immortality, then shall come to pass the saying that is written:
>
> Death is swallowed up in victory.
> O death, where is thy victory?
> O death, where is thy sting?

But thanks be to God, who gives us the victory through our Lord Jesus Christ. (1 Corinthians 15:51–5, 57)

The New Testament speaks of death as 'falling asleep', as easy as that, falling asleep here and waking up there. There is no long sleep, no period of cold storage as it were. The change takes place almost instantaneously, 'in the twinkling of an eye'. Paul says that 'the last trumpet will sound'. I have the feeling and hope that the last trumpet is not the warning or awakening at the consummation at the end of time, centuries or aeons away, but that death itself is the trumpet call, both of warning and summons.

He also tells us that in this process of ageing and dying there is step by step the beginning of new life and renewal:

So we do not lose heart. Though our outer nature is wasting away, our inner nature is being renewed every day. For this slight momentary affliction is preparing for us an eternal weight of glory beyond all comparison, because we look not to the things that are seen but to the things that are unseen; for the things that are seen are transient, but the things that are unseen are eternal. (2 Corinthians 4:16–18)

Many of us may feel that Paul's phrase 'this slight momentary affliction' is hardly applicable to people who are in an agony of pain, dying from cancer. He certainly suffered from some chronic 'thorn in the flesh', but this was not sufficiently disabling to prevent him engaging in three strenuous missionary journeys, nor seemingly was it so painful as to absorb body and mind to the exclusion of all else, making prayer difficult even to holy souls. His mind, as he writes, is on the divine promise of glory beyond all description, easy to understand and believe in in moments of remission and inspiration. What can be said to this?

We can indeed be thankful that the skill and care of doctors can reduce pain to a great degree. We can also be grateful for the growing number of hospices, where patients may be relieved both of physical pain, and of the mental and spiritual problem often associated with it, and so prepared for the great change that takes place in death. The sympathy and fellowship among patients in such hospices, and the faith and care of both trained and voluntary staff, are matters for which patients, relatives and all who learn about this ministry, can thank both those who exercise it and God who directly or unperceivedly inspires it. We may surely apply the promise of our Lord that in as much as we do it to the most suffering of these his brethren and sisters we do it to him.

Teilhard de Chardin has a moving paragraph about the experience of old age:

When the signs of age begin to mark my body (and still more when they touch my mind); when the ill that is to diminish me or carry me off strikes from without or is born within me; when the painful moment comes in which I suddenly awaken to the fact that I am ill or growing old; and above all at that last moment when I feel I am losing hold of myself and am absolutely passive within the hands of the great unknown forces that have formed me; in all those dark moments, O God, grant that I may understand that it is You (provided only my faith is strong enough) who are painfully parting the fibres of my being in order to penetrate to the very marrow of my substance and bear me away within Yourself.[1]

Teilhard also speaks of the need to be hollowed out, so that God can penetrate into our being and fill us with his own life:

God must, in some way or other, make room for Himself, hollowing us out and emptying us, if He is finally to penetrate into us. And in order to assimilate us in Him, He must break the molecules of our being so as to recast and remodel us. The function of death is to provide the necessary entrance into our inmost selves. It will make us undergo the required dissociation. It will put us into the state organically needed if the divine fire is to descend upon us. And in that way its fatal power to decompose and dissolve will be harnessed to the most sublime operations of life.[2]

[1] Quoted in G. Appleton *et al*, *The Human Search*. Fount 1979.
[2] ibid.

Jesus speaks of preparing a place for us, and of coming in his risen being to conduct us into ours:

> Let not your hearts be troubled; believe in God, believe also in me. In my Father's house are many rooms; if it were not so, would I have told you that I go to prepare a place for you? And when I go and prepare a place for you, I will come again and will take you to myself, that where I am you may be also. (John 14:1–3)

Jesus spoke of his own death as going to the Father. His last words were, 'Father, into thy hands I commend my spirit' (Luke 23:46). So death is not going away from home, but going home, though the vanishing from physical sight of our loved ones who die or of ourselves from our loved ones may initially be almost unbearable, until our faith in after life becomes a matter of deep conviction, spiritual sight and unwavering confidence.

I remember with gratitude being present at a funeral in Burma, when the preacher was a senior Burmese priest who gave a very telling parable about death as going home to God, where we belong. He reminded the crowd of mourners and sympathisers of the practice of the cultivators of rice at harvest time. The paddy fields were usually well outside the village, and the farmer or his tenant would build a bamboo hut and stay there until the crop had been cut and winnowed and safely gathered. Then he would leave the temporary hut and go back to his village. As he made his way back he would pass other villagers still at their harvest task, who would call out, 'Where are you going?' His reply would be, 'I am going home', and they would speed him on his way, 'Go well, go well!', knowing that in a few days they would happily do the same.

So dying is a period of transition from this present life into the next, and a preparation for the change.

St Paul in prison in Rome, not knowing whether his trial would result in release or death, tells his people in Philippi that for himself he would rather die, 'for that is far better', but that it may well turn out that he will be released and continue with them for their further progress and increasing joy (Philippians 1:19–26). On the occasion of which Paul is writing he was released, but some years later when Nero was emperor he was imprisoned again and this time he expected to be executed. In a letter to his beloved disciple and fellow-worker he, or someone writing in his faith and spirit, writes:

> For I am already on the point of being sacrificed; the time of my departure has come. I have fought the good fight, I have finished the race, I have kept the faith. Henceforth there is laid up for me the crown of righteousness, which the Lord, the righteous judge, will award to me on that day, and not only to me but also to all who have loved his appearing. (2 Timothy 4:6–8)

Humbly and thankfully we who are entering this period of migration should be able to say the same. A collect which goes back to Pope Gelasius who lived in the fifth century is a gem of comfort, faith and hope:

> O God, who has prepared for those who love Thee such good things as pass man's understanding; pour into our hearts such love toward Thee, that we, loving Thee above all things may obtain thy promises, which exceed all that we can desire. Through our Lord Jesus Christ. Amen.[3]

---

[3] Collect for 6th Sunday after Trinity, Book of Common Prayer.

4

Whispers of Immortality

As we read the Old Testament, which was the only Scripture that Jesus knew, most of us get the idea that people in biblical Israel did believe in some kind of after life, but that it was a shadowy, gloomy existence, considerably inferior to our present life, and certainly not approaching the risen life as understood by writers in the New Testament, who all had the advantage of knowing about the resurrection of Jesus and the assuring experience of his continued spiritual presence.

Some of the psalmists had this hopeless view. The writer of Psalm 6, for example, says: 'For in death there is no remembrance of thee; in Sheol who can give thee praise?' (Psalm 6:5).

Another psalmist asks: 'What profit is there in my death, if I go down to the Pit? Will the dust praise thee? Will it tell of thy faithfulness?' (Psalm 30:9).

The writer of Psalm 88 asks three further questions: 'Dost thou work wonders for the dead? Do the shades rise up to praise thee? Is thy steadfast love declared in the grave, or thy faithfulness in Abaddon? Are thy wonders known in the darkness, or thy saving help in the land of forgetfulness?' (Psalm 88: 10–12). To all three questions the New Testament answers Yes! Yes! Yes!

On the other hand some psalms show glimmers of hope: 'For thou dost not give me up to Sheol, or let thy godly one see the Pit. Thou does show me the path of life; in thy presence is the fulness of joy, in thy right hand are pleasures for evermore' (Psalm 16:10–11). 'As for me, I shall behold thy face in righteousness; when I awake, I shall be satisfied with beholding thy form' (Psalm 17:15).

Psalm 23 gives hope and comfort to many people:

> Even though I walk through the valley of the shadow of death, I fear no evil; for thou art with me; thy rod and staff comfort me. . . . Surely goodness and mercy shall follow me all the days of my life; and I shall dwell in the house of the Lord for ever. (Psalm 23:4,6)

In the original Hebrew of this psalm, the mention is the valley of deep gloom, with the danger of being attacked by lurking enemies or wild animals, so a Jewish commentator says that the psalmist is not thinking of departure from this world. Yet the same commentator speaks of 'the exquisite wording which has become part of religious vocabulary and one hesitates to interfere with it'.[1] Often a later writer puts a fresh interpretation in expanding experience and faith, as in the inspired version quoted, which for many gener-

---

[1] Rabbi Cohen, *The Psalms* (Soncino Press 1945), p. 68.

ations has brought comfort and reassurance to the sick and dying.

The Book of Job, which is a dramatic poem dealing with the problem of the good man who suffers, is also a protest against the conventional view that suffering is a punishment for sin. Its date is thought to be the beginning of the fifth century B.C. At one point he trembles on the threshold of belief in an after life. Cursing the day of his birth he cries out in his sufferings:

> Why was I not as a hidden untimely birth,
>   as infants that never see the light?
> There the wicked cease from troubling,
>   and there the weary are at rest.
> There the prisoners are at ease together;
>   They hear not the voice of the taskmaster.
> The small and the great are there,
>   and the slave is free from his master. (Job 3:16–19)

Later there is an even clearer hint: 'I know that my Redeemer [or Vindicator] lives, and at last he will stand upon the earth; and after my skin has been thus destroyed, then from my flesh I shall see God, whom I shall see on my side, and my eyes shall behold, and not another' (Job 19:25–7).

Yet the vindication is 'upon the earth'; and he believes that 'from the flesh I shall see God'; surely to see God, the Invisible, must be an answer to his troubling problem!

We find more explicit trust and faith in the Book of Wisdom, written in Greek towards the middle of the first century B.C., well after the

persecutions of the second century B.C. when so
many Jews died rather than give up their faith and
culture. It was in pondering over the fate of those
who took part in the Maccabean resistance that
faith in an after life seemed the only possible
explanation. Chapter 3 is perhaps the best known
passage from this book, being read at many
funerals and memorial services:

> The souls of the righteous are in the hand of
> God, and no torment will ever touch them. In
> the eyes of the foolish they seemed to have
> died, and their departure was thought to be an
> affliction, and their going from us to be their
> destruction; but they are at peace. For though
> in the sight of men they were punished, their
> hope is full of immortality.
>
> Having been disciplined a little, they will
> receive great good, because God tested them
> and found them worthy of himself; like gold in
> the furnace he tried them, and like a sacrificial
> burnt offering he accepted them.
>
> Those who trust in him will understand truth,
> and the faithful will abide with him in love,
> because grace and mercy are upon his elect,
> and he watches over his holy ones. (Wisdom
> 3:1–6, 9)

Knowing more of God's mercy and forgiveness,
many would like to add to the souls of the righteous, also the souls of the unrighteous.

The Book of Daniel, written perhaps a century
earlier to encourage those undergoing persecution

for their faith to stand fast, speaks of a resurrection of both righteous and unrighteous.

> Many of those who sleep in the dust of the earth shall awake, some to everlasting life, and some to shame and everlasting contempt. And those who are wise shall shine like the brightness of the firmament; and those who turn many to righteousness, like the stars for ever and ever. (Daniel 12:2–3)

The Book of Isaiah, in a passage probably later than the prophet of that name in Jerusalem, has a more explicit expectation which envisages a physical resurrection: 'Thy dead shall live, their bodies shall rise. O dwellers in the dust awake and sing for joy! For thy dew is a dew of light, and on the land of the shades thou wilt let it fall' (Isaiah 26:19).

By the time of Jesus most Jews had come to believe in life after death. The Sadducees did not, and their attempt to confute Jesus by a subtly devised question may be read in Matthew 22:23–33, which includes our Lord's insights into the resurrection life. Quite recently Pinchas Lapide, an orthodox Jewish rabbi and a close friend of mine devoted to interfaith dialogue and understanding, wrote a book called *The Resurrection of Jesus*[2] which combines a sympathetic and careful study of the subject and the teaching of the New Testament, while maintaining that life after death is part of the Jewish faith experience.

[2] S.P.C.K. 1984.

I have dealt at some length with the development of explicit belief in after life in the Old Testament, for that testament is an essential part of the Christian Bible without which it is almost impossible to understand the experience, faith and teaching of Jesus. Other religions to Judaism and Christianity also believe in an after life. In ancient Egypt people were preoccupied with the question of after life and the cult of the dead, and the massive building of the Pyramids is a symbol of this. In these royal tombs all kinds of vessels and food were provided for the use of the dead pharaoh in the after life. I remember my first visit to Egypt when I was taken to see the interior of the Great Pyramid, and went into the chamber where the pharaoh had been buried and the smaller one where his queen had been interred. Connecting the two chambers was a narrow pipe-like channel, so that the spirits of the dead king and queen could keep in touch with each other. There was also belief in Osiris, the god behind the annual cycle of plant life, the dying of vegetation each winter and its renewal in the spring, symbolising both the dying and the living god. The Egyptian Book of the Dead was a guide book to help people in their future journey and subsequent life, which included an account of judgment to decide whether the dead person was worthy to enter the land of Osiris.

Buddhists believe in reincarnation in a whole series of lives, until at last the repeatedly returning life is fit to enter the final ineffable and indescribable perfection and bliss of Nirvana. Buddhists in Tibet attach great importance to the *Bardo*

Thodol or Book of the Dead which describes the experiences of the individual between death and rebirth.

The Chinese have a practice of ancestor-veneration which may go back to very ancient times, even to 'Peking man' who is thought by archaeologists to have lived 400,000 years ago. The ancestors are interested in the continuance of life and are often consulted about the happenings in human life.

In the tribal religion of Africa belief in ancestors plays an important part. A friend who had worked in Sierre Leone told me that at a certain season in the year non-Christians and Christians alike go to the graveyards and call out: 'Fathers and grandfathers, in a week's time we shall bring you offerings of food and wine. Get ready to receive us.' A study made some years ago in Accra spoke of the custom in which a new-born child is taken out from the hut on the eighth day and introduced to the ancestors, whose blessing is invoked for the new little member of the tribe.

Almost everywhere we hear of people who believe in life after death. What does such belief and experience say to us today?

It does not necessarily prove that there is life after death. It is an indication of a widespread desire for immortality, and a hope for a continuing relationship with those we have known and loved in this life. When people living in isolated communities over many generations, without modern methods of communication, come to similar convictions it may well be something implanted in human nature, arising from our deep self-consciousness.

More deeply still as we ponder the question of a transcendent and immanent God, the Creator who set the whole human process in being, it could well be that he is disclosing himself to those seeking to know the secret of life and immortality. For me the key to the mystery lies in the conviction of Jesus that eternal life comes from knowing God, and the further faith that he has made himself known supremely in Jesus Christ.

Might it not be God whispering in the human heart he created, the intuition of eternal life and the way to it, whispering, as it were, in a spiritual radio to his children, people from every tribe, nation and race under heaven, destined by his grace to pass through the gateway of death into an eternity of life and love!

5

Jesus and Death

As we read the gospels it seems quite clear that Jesus expected death, that he was willing for it, and that he believed that it would be the climax of his ministry and an hour of glory. He also insisted that the when and how lay within his own decision: 'No one takes it from me, but I lay it down of my own accord, I have power to lay it down and I have power to take it again; this charge I have received from my Father' (John 10:18).

I believe that this expectation and willing acceptance of death came to him in the first weeks of his ministry. After his baptism in the Jordan when he heard the Father's voice saying within him, 'Thou art my beloved Son; with thee I am well pleased', he had felt the power of the Spirit coming upon him as convincingly as if a dove had flown down from heaven (Mark 1:10,11). The next forty days he spent in the desert country around Jericho. His object was to find out from the mind of God how to carry out his ministry and win the world to God.

Various possibilities came into his mind – to provide men with material things; to work some

sensational miracle and so compel men to believe;
to compromise possibly with Jewish nationalism
or with the Romans' far-flung imperialism – all of
which he rejected. We are not told what he finally
decided; we can only deduce that from subsequent
insights and happenings. My interpretation is that
Jesus chose the way of love, of service and
sacrifice, and, if necessary, for God's love to be
demonstrated by his own death. Looking back to
the forty days of spiritual travail, we may say that
even at that early stage he could see the shadow
of a cross.

We may ask, 'Did God will Jesus to die? Was
it all pre-determined, fixed and inevitable?' The
quotation from John 10 (above) asserts that it was
not. Reading between the lines of the gospels, it
looks as if God's will was that Jesus should reveal,
in word and action, the love of God and his
forgiveness of men's sinfulness. If they were to
accept those gospel blessings, well and good. If
they should reject them he should still go on exhi-
biting love; if they were to persecute him he was
to continue all the same. If they were to kill him
– which was the worst that they could do – he was
not to fail in love. Later Jesus was to say to his
disciples, as the probability of death increased,
'Greater love has no man than this, that a man
should lay down his life', not only for his friends,
but for those who were plotting and would bring
about his death.

Jesus could have avoided death. He was
tempted to do so. There was the spiritual agony
in Gethsemane, when he sweated blood in the
thought of the physical pain either of stoning by

his fellow-Jews or crucifixion by the Romans. More even than the anticipation of this excruciating suffering was the need of assurance that it was the Father's will. Humanly speaking it would be the end of all his hopes, failure in the task that God had laid upon him. At the end of that agonizing in the garden, he was able to say, 'Not my will, but thine be done!', not in resignation but in glad acceptance. If in the circumstances it was God's will, then he could leave the sequel in God's hands.

An incident recorded in the fourth gospel confirms this interpretation. A few days before his death a group of Greeks from Galilee, probably God-fearers attracted by Jewish faith in God and their dedication to live according to the Torah (Law), came to Philip and Andrew who were from the same region of Decapolis, and asked to be introduced to Jesus. Their coming aroused a deep disturbance in the mind of Jesus. 'Now is my soul troubled,' he said, 'and what shall I say? "Father, save me from his hour?" No, for this purpose I have come to this hour. Father, glorify thy name' (John 12:27–8).

In this incident the possibility of a mission to the world outside Palestine probably came to his mind, where his message would be more welcomed. The issue is decided by an analogy from nature: only if a grain of wheat falls into the earth and dies does it germinate and become a plant with perhaps a hundred grains in the ears that grow from it. Without the death of the seed there can be no crop in nature; similarly there can be no harvest of souls without the death of Jesus.

As in Gethsemane his heart is now at peace, crystallized in the confident words, 'I, when I am lifted up from the earth, will draw all men to myself', and to the Father whose representative he is. Christians see in this crystallized faith, not only a reference to Christ's crucifixion, but also to his exaltation by God to heaven.

The passion of Jesus was to be an hour of glory when the love of God could be shown to the uttermost, to the very end. Death was to him a going to the Father, as evidenced by the last words just before he died, 'Father, into thy hands I commend my spirit' (Luke 23:46). His confidence in life after death both for himself and others, was shown in his words to the friendly thief, 'Today you will be with me in Paradise', the last word in that assurance conjuring up a vision of a quiet garden, with release from pain, a place of peace and refreshment.

Before he died, Jesus felt within himself that he had completed the task that God had laid upon him. Throughout his ministry, through months of growing opposition, through the last days of the now certainty of death, through the last hours of physical agony and mental anguish, his faith and love had not failed. So before the last quiet words of trust he could shout for all to hear, 'It is finished!', a cry of relief certainly, but not of despair, rather of triumph. The task given him by God has been completed. God's love and his own love have been shown to the uttermost. His forgiveness and God's forgiveness have been shown in the worst suffering and in death. For the first time in human history a man has been completely obedient to God's Will. He is completely one with the Father in heart and will. He is also completely human, so that the love of God can flow through him into the whole human race.

The moment of Christ's death was the greatest moment of his life, when he went to the Father. We may reverently imagine the Father's welcome as he was clasped to the Father's heart and heard again the Father's words, 'You are truly my beloved Son, in you I am well pleased!'

The moment of death was not only the going to the Father. It was also the moment of resurrection, the moment of ascension, the moment of expansion to become what nowadays we speak of as a cosmic force, to be present everywhere and always with God himself, who penetrates and permeates his whole creation. Henceforth he would affect the totality of mankind, the whole of the universe, every succeeding and past generation, no longer limited by time, space and physical confinement.

The New Testament speaks of a three days interval between the death of Jesus and his resurrection. The Bible uses this term not as the equivalent of seventy-two hours in our measure of time but as the time between an act of God and its apprehension by us humans. In a similar way forty days seems a mystical term indicating the time of preparation before an act of God can be followed up and worked out in human history and made universally relevant and effective. So I am led to think of the death of Christ at a certain moment on the first Good Friday as also including the festivals of Easter and Ascension in a glorious divine simultaneity.

We can never exhaust the significance of Christ's death. For the first time in human history a man, as human as each of us, had lived and died one in mind, heart and will with the Father: the first perfect man, 'the first-born among many brethren' (Romans 8:29). The grace of God could have uninterrupted flow in him and through him, until it reaches each one of us today. We must be grateful to John Hick for summing up in one clear, all-embracing sentence: 'The result of this is that the Christ-spirit, restricted during the period of the incarnation to exerting an influence in one place at a time, is now able to influence the world as a whole, changing the environment in which men have ever since lived.'[1]

We can gratefully agree with St John that the hour of Christ's death is indeed an hour of glory, and express our gratitude in a prayer of Dean Milner-White's:

> Blessed be the hour, O Christ, in which thou was born,
>   and the hour in which thou didst die:
> Blessed be the dawn of thy rising again,
>   and the high day of thine ascending:
> O most merciful and mighty Redeemer Christ,
>   let all times be the time of our presence with thee,
>   and of thy dwelling with us.[2]

---

[1] John Hick, *Death and Eternal Life*. Collins 1976.
[2] Eric Milner-White, *My God My Glory*. S.P.C.K. 1967.

6

Our Death

Jesus not only took his disciples into his confidence about his own expectation of death, his own willingness to undergo death and his conviction that only his death would convince people of God's unlimited love and his own love to the end and to the uttermost, but also stressed the effective consequence of personal trust in him and acceptance of his teaching:

> Truly, truly, I say to you, he who hears my word and believes him who sent me, has eternal life; he does not come into judgment, but has passed from death to life. Truly, truly, I say to you, the hour is coming, and now is, when the dead will hear the voice of the Son of God, and those who hear will live. (John 5:24–5).

Three gospel incidents tell us of three people, apparently dead, who were able to hear his voice and were resuscitated to continuing physical life. The first was the daughter of Jairus, a ruler of the synagogue at Capernaum. She had been 'dead' for only a few minutes before Jesus arrived at her bedside. Taking her by the hand, he said, '*Talitha cumi'*, 'Little one, arise', and the twelve-year-old got up and walked, to the amazement and joy of her parents and the three watching disciples (Mark 5:21–4, 35–41).

The second example is that of the widow's son at Nain, who had been dead for some hours and whose body was being carried to the graveyard. Jesus, seeing the mother's grief, halted the bearers and called to the dead man, 'Young man, I say to you, arise', whereupon the dead man sat up and began to speak (Luke 7:11–17).

The third incident was the reanimation of Lazarus, a dear friend of Jesus whose body had been in the burial cave four days. Jesus called in a loud voice, 'Lazarus, come out!' and the dead man, still in his funeral wrappings, staggered out and had his bandages unbound by awe-struck friends (John 11:38–44).

All three heard the voice of Jesus, obeyed it and were restored to physical life, not yet to the eternal life promised by Jesus to believers.

Ladislaus Boros distinguishes the various kinds of death, linking recent discovery with gospel experience:

(1) *Clinical death* denotes the act of dying in which the cessation of the essential bodily functions occurs. This in no way means that 'the separation of the soul from the body' has already taken place.

(2) *Relative death* describes the state obtaining after the cessation of function has lasted for some length of time. The soul can no longer express itself through the body, and, unless

some quite extraordinary clinical operation – or a miracle – occurs, the body is incapable of being reanimated.

(3) *Absolute death* is the moment when 'the soul leaves the body'. Existence is released from the condition of temporariness and attains its definitive state of being. It is at this moment, which we can describe metaphysically but cannot determine physically, that the final decision is made.[1]

In a discussion with Jews from Jerusalem and his own listening disciples and friends, Jesus says: 'Truly, truly, I say to you, if any one keeps my word he will never *see* death', the implication being that the eternal life growing within him will be so strong that he will hardly notice death when it comes. A little later in this encounter, there is a slightly different refutation: 'If any one keeps my word, he will never taste death', suggesting that the believer will hardly feel death, he will take it in his stride (John 8:51–2).

Before the Lazarus resuscitation Jesus says to Martha (not Mary): 'I am the resurrection and the life, he who believes in me, though he die, yet shall he live, and whoever lives and believes in me shall never die' (John 11:25–6). The first 'die' in this text clearly refers to physical dying, and the second to spiritual death.

St John's Gospel with its spiritual interpretations puts together both his actual memories of

[1] L. Boros, *The Moment of Truth* (Search Press 1972), p. 172.

our Lord's incarnate life, and his experience of
the Risen Christ through the next fifty or more
years.

I have already quoted our Lord's saying that we
should not fear those who kill the body but cannot
kill the soul, and his warning that there is one
who can destroy both body and soul in hell, which
to my mind must mean the devil. The first type
of murderer can only inflict physical death, the
second has the power to kill both body and soul
in hell. This cannot be God, for he is a God of
mercy who does not desire the death of the sinner.
The devil will kill the spiritual life as well, if we
allow him to do so.

The Jewish Christian writer of the Epistle to
the Hebrews also deals with the widespread fear
of death: 'Christ himself partook of our nature,
that through death he might destroy him who has
the power of death, that is the devil, and deliver
all those who through fear of death were subject
to lifelong bondage' (Hebrews 2:14–15). The
writer appeals to his readers for faith, as Jesus
does in the gospels:

> Therefore, brethren, since we have confidence
> to enter the sanctuary by the blood of Jesus, by
> the new and living way which he opened for us
> through the curtain, that is, through his flesh,
> and since we have a great high priest over the
> house of God, let us draw near in full assurance
> of faith. (Hebrews 10:19–22)

In the Revelation to John, the writer speaks of
his own experience of the Risen Christ and his

own assurance that faith in him will unlock the mystery of death and hell: 'Fear not, I am the first and the last, and the living one; I died, and behold I am alive for evermore, and I have the keys of Death and Hades' (Revelation 1:17–18).

So with us as with Jesus, there need be no fear of death, whether we are thinking of ourselves or about the fate of loved ones who have physically died. The hour of death can be an hour of glory, and by facing it with quiet confidence we can make it an act of ever-growing closer to God and to his beloved, loving, perfect Son, Jesus the Christ.

Anyone who has kept the dead body of a loved one in the house during the days before the funeral, leaving the face uncovered, and from time to time comes into the room to look at the closed eyes, the folded hands, and perhaps kiss the cold brow, realises that the animating spirit has left the body through which it expressed its self. Yet the mourner may be conscious of the spirit hovering near, eager to speak to the one left. If he or she gets such a glimpse, would it not be right to speak in the hope and belief that the hovering spirit can hear what is being said? Ought not this seemingly one-sided conversation to go on every day, when I, as it were, tell her of the happenings of the past day, and listen in silence for a few minutes of spiritual continuing interest and care?

I have sometimes felt a presence as I drift into sleep or slowly wake to consciousness after the night's rest, as if someone were sitting by my bedside.

We need to know nothing except that God is.

My loved one and I are always in his sight. We meet there, and the heart of the mourning one is warmed, and the heart of the seemingly hidden one may equally be warmed and assured of loving remembrance and of a longing for spiritual sight and hearing in this caress of the heart.

The Paraphernalia of Death

Most people have attended at least one funeral, perhaps that of the body of a dearly loved relation or friend of many years, or of someone they had admired, or possibly out of sympathy with the bereaved family. Often the members of the family think of the funeral as the farewell instead of their last visit to the dying.

The funeral is really the reverent disposal of the worn out and deserted body. Arnold Toynbee says:

> However diverse man's funerary rites have been, they have all had a common signification. They have signified that a human being has a dignity in virtue of his being human; that his dignity survives his death; and that therefore his dead body must not simply be treated as garbage and be thrown away like the carcase of a dead non-human creature, or like a human being's worn-out boots or clothes.[1]

---

[1] A. Toynbee (ed.), *Man's Concern with Death* (Hodder 1968), p. 60.

41

As one sits in the church or crematorium waiting for the service to begin, memory recalls one's own relationship with the one who has died, often with gratitude or admiration, sometimes with relief that long months of physical pain are over, sometimes in the case of younger people or children with regret that they have not had a longer time to enjoy the wonder and beauty of the world and the joy of loving relationships. Often the thought of our own mortality will come to mind, leaving us somewhat disturbed and uneasy.

Sometimes the officiating priest will have been on cemetery duty most of the day, and rather tiredly recites the set words, with professional solemnity but no great sensitivity for the sad and confused mourners. Some years ago I wrote two short prayers to stir the right pastoral feeling in my heart:

O Lover of Souls, grant me your eternal love, as I stand by the bedside of the dying. Without your love, I am at the best only doing my duty. Speak through my words and through my silence, through your delegated love, a word of comfort, trust, and expectant hope and joy. O home of every heart.

O Ever-living Christ, don't let me be just a functional priest, but one also who believes with you the Father's will of continuing life and love, the assurance of forgiveness and the hope of continuing growth in love and holiness.

Funerals are often sad and depressing, instead of being, if our faith is true, occasions of loving remembrance, quiet trust, and even joy that the spirit of the dead body has moved on to the next stage which God in his providence has prepared.

In my first curacy in East London, sixty years ago, drawn blinds, funeral tolling, black clothes, armbands, widow's veils, scores of wreaths, and a feeling that grief must be adequately expressed, was the accepted thing. All this was certainly not as tragic and sad as portrayed by the famous hymn writer John Mason Neale, who on the way to his uncle's funeral in 1839 wrote the following poem:

Oh, give us back the days of old! Oh! give me
                     back an hour!
To make us feel that Holy Church o'er death
                   hath might and power.
Take hence the heathen trappings, take hence
                   the Pagan show,
The misery, the heartlessness, the unbelief of
                       woe:
The nodding plumes, the painted staves, the
                   mutes in black array,
That get their hard-won earnings by so much
                   grief per day:
The steeds and scarves and crowds that gaze
                 with half-suspended breath
As if, of all things terrible, most terrible was
                      death:
And let us know to what we go, and wherefore
                 we must weep,
Or o'er the Christian's hopeful rest, or
                 everlasting sleep.

Lay in the dead man's hand the Cross – the
                    Cross upon his breast
Because beneath the shadow of the Cross he
                    went to rest:
And let the Cross go on before – the Crucified
                    was first
To go before the people and their chains of
                    death to burst;
And be the widow's heart made glad with
                    charitable dole,
And pray with calm yet earnest faith for the
                    departed soul.
And be the *De Profundis* said for one of
                    Christ's own fold,
And – for a prisoner is set free – the bells be
                    rung not tolled.
When face to face we stand with death, thus
                    Holy Church records,
He is our slave, and we, through Her, his
                    masters and his lords.
Deck the High Altar for the Mass! Let tapers
                    guard the hearse!
For Christ, the Light that lighteneth all, to
                    blessing turns our curse,
And be Nicea's Creed intoned and be the
                    Gospel read,
In calm, low voice, for preaching can profit
                    not the dead.
Then forth with banner, cross, and psalm, and
                    chant, and hymn and prayer,
And look not on the coffin – for our brother
                    is not there;
His soul, we trust assuredly, is safe in
                    Abraham's breast,

And mid Christ's many faithful, his body shall
                                    have rest.
When earth its cares and turmoils, and many
                              sorrows cease –
By all thy woes, by all thy joys, Lord Jesus
                              grant them peace.[2]

James Frazer in his great book *The Golden
Bough*, published in 1900, speaks of the funeral
customs of primal people, who certainly believed
in the continued life of the spirits of the dead, but
told also of the fear of them, as if the spirit of
the loving grandfather or grandmother at death
turned into a harming character. I remember
hearing of a custom of the Kachins, an animistic
tribe in North Burma, in which a rope ladder
would be let down into the grave and the spirit
priest would address the dead person by name,
and bid him come up the ladder, go to the north
through the forest, crossing any stream where a
length of cotton would be stretched across (for
spirits were thought of as not being able to cross
water) and remain in the mountains of the dead,
and under no circumstances come back to disturb
the village. Burma being a tropical country,
funerals took place within twenty-four hours of
death. Often I was present and ready for the
funeral, but if a night intervened all the village
people would sit up, singing to keep awake,
apparently lest the spirit should want to enter the

[2] Quoted in Geoffrey Rowell, *Hell and the Victorians*.
Oxford 1974.

body of anyone present instead of going off to the place of the dead.

Many of us have read Evelyn Waugh's novel of American grief, *The Loved One*, in which he describes methods of embalming to keep the dead body from decaying until the day of resurrection, or possibly until some hoped for elixir of life is discovered, regardless of Paul's warning that 'flesh and blood cannot inherit the kingdom of God, nor does the perishable inherit the imperishable . . . but we shall all be changed' (1 Corinthians 15:50, 51).

I often wish we could find a more positive, meaningful word for those who have died than 'dead', a word generally associated with the corpse, so still, lifeless and cold, so quickly decaying and to all appearances quite finished. Some of us use the word 'departed', but that suggests gone away. Some friends of mine have thought that 'the arrived' would be more meaningful than 'the departed', but this suggestion still conveys the idea of separation, 'there' though not also 'here'. Others speak of 'passed on' but that too suggests absence. Some talk of 'falling asleep' and mystery writers talk of 'the long sleep', both indicating inactivity, almost cold storage. 'The late lamented' is often used in journalistic reports but I find myself more reluctant to use that term than any already mentioned.

I have spoken to many friends about finding the right word. Several have suggested 'the unseen ones', and this certainly suggests a sense of presence. The best suggestion to date comes from a friend nearly as old as myself, who speaks of 'the risen ones'.

We also tend to speak loosely about the disposal of the body – 'he was buried last week', 'she will be cremated on Friday' – perhaps only a shorthand way of speaking of the funeral, and in any case implying that our attention is more on the dead body than the living spirit.

It is perhaps understandable that grieving relatives or friends should associate the grave with the person as well as the corpse, and that therefore a visit to the grave seems in some way a resumption of personal contact. Would not this be, however, a relationship with the past rather than with the present, a static memory rather than a dynamic ongoing hope? One would hesitate to speak in an insensitive way about visits to graves in the Falklands or to vast cemeteries in Normandy, and named tombstones do witness to individual identity. Perhaps the sounding of the Reveille immediately after the Last Post has a note of inspiration that we do not always notice. The silent attention at the grave of the Unknown Warrior in many countries can make us hope, as well as urge us to abolish war which cuts off numberless young men and women, and even children, just as they are advancing to fruitfulness and maturity. I must not concentrate too exclusively on human experiences and reactions. For God is the God of hope, my faith and thought must be on him, from consciousness of the human start, through all the changing scenes of life, to the divine finish. As we stand at the open grave or visit a churchyard or plant spring bulbs or forget-me-nots at some memory-stirring little garden, it may be that there will be a whisper in the heart, such as the faithful women heard on the first Easter morning: 'The one you love is not here. The one you love is risen!'

8

The Spiritual and the Psychical

Almost everywhere there is a new and deep interest in the inner life of mankind. This is partly due to the discoveries of the great psychologists such as Freud, Jüng and Adler, partly due to the saintly paleontologist and thinker, Teilhard de Chardin, who urged people to study man as a phenomenon, while at the same time going deep into his own spiritual life, relating it to the divine milieu or environment; paralleled by the scholarly studies of the biologist Sir Alister Hardy in his search for meaning and immanence in all life, and later in the Religious Experience Research Unit which he founded, giving the first results of such research in *The Spiritual Nature of Man.*[1] Religious communities, Roman, Anglican, Orthodox and lay, have made a great contribution to the understanding and practice of the spiritual life. Naturally the questions of ageing, dying and life after death are subjects for their own meditation and intercession.

The founding of the Society for Psychical Research in 1882 by a group of friends, mainly

[1] Oxford University Press 1983.

Cambridge philosophers and scientists, quickened the interest from the human angle. Study of the paranormal, meaning that beyond normal explanation, and the more explicit agenda of parapsychology which includes telepathy, precognition, mysticism, clairvoyance, clairaudience and psychokinesis, began to be taken seriously. The last item included interesting speculation about poltergeist activity – the strange and inexplicable happenings in a house, noises, creaks, footsteps, the apparent movement of objects, which puzzle people and awaken curiosity and in some cases fear.

Religious people cannot ignore such experiences and interpretations which may be thought of as the quest for the transcendent in and through the paranormal. Thus in 1953 the Churches' Fellowship for Psychical and Spiritual Research was founded, and issues a quarterly journal, *The Christian Parapsychologist.* In recent years some of the churches have appointed commissions to examine these experiences and studies and suggest attitudes and guidelines for their members.

More recently an increasing number of people suddenly stricken by heart attacks and to all appearances clinically dead, have been reanimated by 'the kiss of life' or injections into the heart. Quite a number of them have spoken of these 'near death' experiences, describing how they looked down on their inert bodies, with worried relatives or doctors and nurses around with whom they wanted to speak, and perhaps did but were unable to attract attention. An elderly friend of mine told me of such an experi-

ence. She said that she had had such a feeling of
peace and happiness that she felt sorry to be
brought back, adding that she would never again
be afraid of death.

I have never been intimate enough to talk with
anyone who has deliberately taken an overdose
of drugs. Perhaps some were glad to be 'brought
back', realizing that the overdose was a sudden
mistaken act. Perhaps some with a religious back-
ground felt themselves almost commanded to
return to the unfinished task of life.

Almost all those who have lost someone very
dear want to keep in touch, and some have sought
the help of spiritualist mediums in the hope of
doing so. I have only once attended a seance and
my chief memory of that occasion was the trivial
nature of the presumed messages. Yet I can
believe that there are genuine 'sensitives', though
I have not yet had the privilege of getting to know
one. What I would love to discover would be
something that could be available for everyone, a
sensitivity to the spiritual, arising out of
continuing love, daily intercession and a conviction that those I long to keep in touch with are
equally eager to keep in touch with me.

At the present time there is a disturbing interest
in occult powers and magic, accompanied by
ceremonies which come close in outward appear-
ance to Christian worship. Adherents of the main
traditions of religious faith all warn against being
involved in these. Such ideas and practices are
likely to spread unless there is clear teaching and
critical discrimination on the part of religious
bodies. In the 1662 ordination of priests the candi-

dates are reminded by the presiding bishop that they are called to be messengers, watchmen and stewards, bringing messages from God, watching and warning lest any evil should threaten the individual or corporate spiritual life, for example superstitious ideas or self-seeking motives; and at the same time being channels of God's protecting and supporting grace.

In our thoughts about death and dying the question of 'reincarnation' often arises. I have met a number of people who claim to have knowledge of past lives, and who hope to return to this life again. In Burma I duly studied the twelve great birth stories and the 550 lesser reincarnations of the Buddha, for whom I have a great affection and something approaching reverence. Yet I also remember that the teaching of the Buddha was to live a life of virtue now, in order to escape from the spiral of rebirth into the sphere of unknowing, the sphere of ultimate perfection and beatitude, the indescribable peace of Nirvana.

Some people have spoken to me of spiritual guides whom they believe advise them in every step of this life. I must confess that I do not yearn for some Red Indian chief or Indian guru or Middle East djinn; but I would welcome some saintly priest who has helped me in earlier years, or any writer from past centuries whose books gave me a new insight into holy living and dying; and I would thrill with joy if my companion in over fifty years of married love who knows me better than any other human being was able to advise and guide me. Above all I joyfully believe in the omnipresence of the Risen Christ and from time to time experience a quiet peace and happiness, and inspiring thoughts pour into my mind so quickly that I hardly have time to register them.

When a person facing death knows intuitively that it is near he may try to keep this knowledge from his family. On the other hand, they may already know from the doctor's prognosis that death cannot be long delayed but may try to reassure him that he will recover. The question arises whether or not the sick person should be told that death is near. It seems to me that there can be no hard and fast rule. Some people live such quiet trusting lives, even in serious sickness, taking each day as it comes. Others are more inquiring and would be grateful to know, so that they can tidy up their affairs and prepare trustingly for the moment of transition. If the sick person raises the question it would seem right to talk about it to relieve their minds from fear, speaking of our common faith that God has prepared good things for the future, without anticipating any mourning of our own.

I am often asked if I believe that when the day of our death comes it has been fixed by God. I usually reply that I believe death will come about by natural causes, but that God will be in it and with us, so that death may be taken in our stride, hardly noticeable.

Some dying people find themselves thinking with clarity of dead friends and are happy in the thought of renewing sight and touch. A few may have a vision of a loved one coming at the moment of death to companion them to the new order of being.

I remember a missionary friend who worked among the Kachin people in Upper Burma telling me of a most moving experience. He had been regularly visiting a village in the Kachin Hills, taking an interest in the people and bringing a stock of medicines for any who were sick. He told them of God's love as revealed in Christ but nobody wanted to become a Christian, until at last a boy of twelve asked to be baptized. Together they went to ask permission of the boy's parents but for a long time they refused. Every time my friend came to the village the little lad would persist with his request. Finally the parents ungraciously gave in, saying, 'Don't be surprised if the spirits become angry and bring sickness and misfortune'. So K'maw Gam was baptized. Shortly afterwards he fell ill and parents and neighbours said it was a punishment from the spirits. But they had the sense to send messengers on the rather long journey to the missionary's headquarters. My friend hastily gathered the simple medicines he always took with him and hurried back to the village to nurse the lad. He told me that he prayed as he had never prayed before that God would show his power and heal K'maw Gam. But he died, and my friend said he felt that God had let him down, and he returned sick at heart to his headquarters. Some weeks later he saw a party of the villagers coming through his garden gate. With a sigh he went to meet them and before he could ask what they wanted, they burst out, 'Teacher, please send teachers to our village!' 'What has changed your minds?' he asked. 'A few weeks ago you were cursing me for little K'maw Gam's death, and now you ask for teachers.' 'Yes, teacher,' was the reply, 'you know that we live in fear of the spirits and are afraid to die, but K'maw Gam, when he died, had a smile on his face, as if he were greeting someone he loved very much. Please send us a teacher!'

My friend's story reminded me of the Negro spiritual sung in the West Indies:

> I looked over Jordan and what did I see
>   coming for to carry me home?
> A band of angels coming after me,
>   coming for to carry me home.
> Swing low, sweet chariot,
>   Coming for to carry me home.

The gospel of death is as simple as that, transmigration to the eternal home which God has prepared for them that love him, and I hope and believe for those also who do not yet love him.

9

Moment of Truth

Death strips us of everything, as Job realized
when he said, 'Naked I came from my mother's
womb, and naked I shall return' (Job 1:21). Paul
had the same thought in mind: 'We brought
nothing into the world, and we cannot take
anything out of the world' (1 Timothy 6:7). In
death we are stripped of everything: money and
possessions, position and honour, ceremonial
garments and university degrees, everything we
thought of as essential and valuable. We are
reduced to our common humanity – kings, states-
men, ecclesiastical dignitaries, millionaires and
beggars, warders and prisoners, judges and
judged.

In death we stand naked before God 'to whom
all hearts are open, all desires known and from
whom no secrets are hidden', transparent before
the God of burning holiness.

At death we shall see ourselves as we really are.
It will be a moment of judgment – self-judgment,
not the confused prisoner in the divine dock anxi-
ously awaiting the verdict of God the Judge of all,
but one who perhaps for the first time sees himself
as he really is. In John's vision of the hereafter

he sees 'the dead, great and small, standing before the throne, and books were opened . . . and the dead were judged by what was written in the books, by what they had done' (Revelation 20:12). It is not the book of life containing the names of those saved so far, for that book is mentioned separately. It has been suggested that the accusing books are the books of memory and character, remembrance of past sins unforgiven and unrepented, and the realization of the kind of people we really are. In the parable of Lazarus and the rich man, Dives is bidden by Father Abraham, 'Son, remember . . .' (Luke 16:25). Without the continuing faculty of memory of past sins there cannot be this self-knowledge and conviction.

In the parable there is also recognition. Dives in Hades recognizes Lazarus. Although there is a great gulf fixed, across which it is not possible to pass, yet there is communication. Dives is able to speak to Abraham and Lazarus presumably to overhear the conversation. Jesus himself as he tells the parable has not yet died. When he does die the barrier which has been hitherto thought impassable is crossed. When Jesus dies, the thief whom we speak of as penitent is able to pass with him into some kind of after life.

May we not also see some signs of hope? The unfortunate Dives is still addressed by Abraham as 'son'. In his anxiety lest his five brothers 'also come into this place of torment' may we not see a glimmer of improvement? As John hints in another context, a greater than Abraham is here (John 8:53). Peter in his first epistle says, 'For this is why the gospel was preached even to the dead, that though judged in the flesh like men, they live in the spirit like God' (1 Peter 4:6). He also speaks of Christ who has died going to preach to the spirits in prison, mentioning particularly those in the time of Noah who were so wicked that the writer of Genesis 6:1–7 imagined God grieved to the heart and sorry that he had created them.

Writers in the New Testament believe that God has entrusted the final judgment to the Risen and Glorified Christ: 'The Father judges no one, but has given all judgment to the Son' (John 5:22). Yet John asserts, 'God so loved the world that He gave his only Son, that whoever believes in him should not perish but have eternal life' (John 3:16), adding, 'For God sent not his Son into the world to condemn the world, but that the world might be saved through him' (John 3:17).

If Christ is to be the final judge, there is hope, for as the writer of the Epistle to the Hebrews says: 'We have not a high priest who is unable to sympathize with our weaknesses, but one who in every respect has been tempted even as we are, yet without sinning' (Hebrews 4:15). He who prayed at a moment of excruciating pain and heartbreaking dereliction, 'Father, forgive them, for they know not what they do' (Luke 23:34), making excuse for all who had a hand in his death, can be trusted to judge with mercy, rather than with merciless justice. Yet there is in Jesus no hint of compromise with evil or of condonation. To the woman caught in adultery and in danger of being stoned he says, 'Neither do I condemn you; go and do not sin again' (John 8:11). Sin is so destroying the souls that God is creating that it must be opposed.

Even John, the apostle of love, speaks of the wrath of God: 'He who believes in the Son has eternal life: he who does not obey the Son shall not see life, but the wrath of God rests upon him' (John 3:36). Paul writing to the Christians in Rome says, 'For the wrath of God is revealed from heaven against all ungodliness and wickedness of men, who by their wickedness suppress the truth' (Romans 1:18). He warns the Christians in Ephesus, 'Let no one deceive you with empty words, for it is because of these things that the wrath of God comes upon the sons of disobedience' (Ephesians 5:6). He is more explicit in his letter to the Colossians: 'Put to death therefore what is earthly in you: immorality, impurity, passion, evil desire, and covetousness, which is idolatry. On account of these the wrath of God is coming' (Colossians 3:5–6).

It is in the Book of Revelation that there is the most emphatic mention of God's wrath. The writer speaks of 'the wine of God's wrath, poured unmixed into the cup of his anger . . . with fire and brimstone' (14:10), and of an angel swinging his sickle and gathering a harvest of the earth which he throws into the great winepress of the wrath of God (14:19). He speaks too of seven last plagues 'with which the wrath of God is ended' (15:1). Nor dare we overlook his vision of one called Faithful and True and the Word of God who will 'smite the nations, and will rule them with a rod of iron, and tread the winepress of the

fury of the wrath of God the Almighty'
(19:11–16).

What can we make of such passages when we
accept our Lord's revelation of God's righteousness and love in the gospels, or read thankfully of
the new heaven and earth and the worship of
heaven and the triumph of good, in other chapters
of the Revelation to John? Sometimes I wonder
if the final editor of that book has included
material from Jewish apocalyptical writings along
with more specifically Christian material.

A more acceptable interpretation may be that
the phrase 'the wrath of God' does not mean the
vindictive, destroying, unrestrained anger of men,
but God's unrelenting opposition to evil, which is
damaging his created children so tragically and
eternally. God surely must be opposed to us as
long as we persist in the destructiveness of sin.
But he is always longing for us to repent, to turn
from our evil ways; he, like his perfect son, is
always seeking the sheep lost through its own fool-
ishness, the coin lost by accident, the son gone
into the far country of wilfulness for whose return
he waits ready with the ring and the shoes and
the best robe and the family meal of celebration,
all ready and waiting (Luke 15).

The first disciples once asked Jesus if there were
many being saved. His reply was that there were
more hurrying thoughtlessly down the wide road
leading to spiritual death, than on the narrow road
leading to eternal life. Yet he said also that he
had compassion on the mass of humanity, who
were like sheep without a shepherd to guide,
guard and feed them.

Paul told his son in faith, Timothy, that 'God our Saviour desires all men to be saved and come to the knowledge of the truth' (1 Timothy 2:3–4). Matthew in his version of the lost sheep adds, 'It is not the will of my Father who is in heaven that one of these little ones should perish' (Matthew 18:14).

Let two quotations from modern writers comfort any troubled heart. The first is from a hymn by F. W. Faber (1814–63):

There's a wideness in God's mercy,
    Like the wideness of the sea;
There's a kindness in his justice,
    Which is more than liberty.

There is no place where earth's sorrows
    Are more felt than up in heaven;
There is no place where earth's failings
    Have such kindly judgment given.[1]

The second comfortable word comes from Father Ladislaus Boros who assures us:

No one is damned merely by chance, because he was suddenly called to eternity by an accident, or because he was born into a family where he never knew what love is and so could never understand what God himself is . . . or because he was hated, rejected, misjudged and wounded to the heart by human beings and so rebelled against everything, including God.[2]

[1] English Hymnal, no. 499.
[2] L. Boros, *Living Hope* (Search Press 1971), p. 26.

We can trust the God and Father of Jesus Christ, who wants all his children, in every generation, to be perfected and eternally blessed.

10

Lord of the Last Things

In almost every service of worship we Christians
are called upon to confess our faith in God,
creator of heaven and earth; in Jesus Christ who
revealed the love of God and by his death in love
for all mankind saves us from our sins; and in the
Holy Spirit who indwells men and sanctifies us.
Nowhere are we called upon to believe that God
creates hell-fire, endless punishment and eternal
death. Some writers in the Bible warn us that
there are such things, and down the ages some
Christians have believed that God will inflict this
fate on unbelievers and unrepentant sinners.

I have always hoped, believed and prayed that
this would not be the case. Yet I have always
feared that there is a hell and that the pains of it
are as painful to the spirit as burning is to the
physical body. But I cannot believe that God
creates hell, and when recently I read in *The
Marriage of East and West* by Bede Griffiths,[1] a
monk living in an Ashram in South India, the
unequivocal statement that the doctrine of everlasting punishment is surely the most terrible

---

[1] Collins 1982.

doctrine ever preached by any religion, my heart thrilled with relief and joy.

So I feel confirmed in my own intuition that God did not and does not create hell. The question of who does create hell must, however, be asked. May not the answer to that question be simply that we make our own hell?

There is a prior question which needs to be answered – what is hell? Jesus in his great prayer offered before he and his disciples moved from the Upper Room to the Garden of Gethsemane said, 'This is eternal life that they know thee, the only God, and Jesus Christ whom thou hast sent' (John 17:3). If heaven is the knowledge of God, then hell must be the failure or refusal to recognize and live in that relationship. Nicolas Berdyaev (1873–1948), a Russian philosopher and author, originally a sceptic of Marxist leanings, found his way back to the Orthodox Church and from 1922 lived in Paris. In *The Destiny of Man*, published in 1937, he says, 'Hell is the state of the soul powerless to come out of itself, absolute self-centredness, dark and evil isolation', that is, final inability to love. He adds that it is not to be envisaged as 'God's action upon the soul, retributive and punitive as that action may be; it is the absence of any action of God upon the soul, the soul's incapacity to open itself to God's influence and its complete severance from God'.[2]

The writer of the Epistle to the Hebrews says that we should 'offer to God acceptable worship

---

[2] Quoted in Geoffrey Rowell, *Hell and the Victorians*. Oxford 1974.

with reverence and awe, for our God is a consuming fire' (Hebrews 12:28–9). This seems to say to me that he does not burn men's souls but the evil that gets alloyed with them, for as the prophet Malachi said, 'The Lord whom you seek will suddenly come to his temple . . . like a refiner's fire . . . purifying his worshippers, refining them like gold and silver (Malachi 3:1–3). The fire is a purifying one; when it has done its work of purification, then it gives light to our minds, warms our hearts, supplies energy to the will, and cuts through difficulties as physical fire cuts through steel.

Berdyaev also saw that to believe in hell is to believe in man's spiritual freedom; man is free to choose. 'Man', he said, 'has a moral right to hell', meaning that God respects and honours the freedom which is an ingredient in man's creation. A wrong choice, an obstinate insistence on evil, hatred, lovelessness, will ultimately lead to the death of the self. To cut one's self off from God is spiritual suicide. To refuse the grace, love and forgiveness which God is always offering is spiritual starvation. To be alienated from God is to be shut up in despair.

On the other hand, man may accept Christ's revelation of God, and follow him to God in life, in physical death and in the life after death. The choice is always ours.

Moses in his last appeal to Israel before they entered the promised land says:

I call heaven and earth to witness against you this day, that I have set before you life and death, blessing and curse, therefore choose life, that you and your descendants may live, loving the Lord your God, obeying his voice and cleaving to Him: for that means life to you. (Deuteronomy 30:19–20)

In the moment of death, as we pass from the material and physical world into the promised land of the spiritual and eternal, we are called upon to choose and decide.

If we choose aright, we shall grow in our relationship to God. Seeing ourselves as we really are we shall recognize that further sanctification is needed, we shall become more conscious of his presence, feel progressively more at home in the divine milieu, until we enjoy the beatitude promised in the sermon on the mount and see God. In the longing words of one of the psalmists, 'As for me, I shall behold thy face in righteousness; when I awake I shall be satisfied with beholding thy form' (Psalm 17:15).

But what if I do not choose and decide aright? Some modern Roman Catholic writers who have written hopefully about the meaning of death, believe that a final choice is made in death, and that after death there is no further chance either of decision or of growth in holiness. I hope and pray that this is not the case. There are so many people in the world who have never experienced love, whose heredity, childhood and environment have never given them a chance: there are those cut off by starvation and disease before they have had any hope of reasonable physical life, those killed anonymously in war, by the bomb planted under a car or by the terrorist's bullet. God is the Lord of mercy and love. As the writer of the Book of Wisdom, written in the interval between the two Testaments, says:

> For Thou lovest all the things that are and abhorrest nothing which thou hast made: for never wouldest Thou have made any thing if Thou hadst hated it. And how could anything have endured, if it had not been thy will? or been preserved, if not called by Thee? But Thou sparest all: for they are thine, O Lord, Thou lover of souls. (Wisdom 11:24–6 A.V.)

And I echo the prayer of Pierre Teilhard de Chardin:

> I pray, O Master, that the flames of hell may not touch me nor any of those whom I love, and even that they may never touch anyone (and I know, my God, that you will forgive this bold prayer).[3]

And I find my own intuition strengthened that the flames of hell are ignited by ourselves and kept burning by our failure to accept the forgiveness of God which can quench every fiery furnace.

But having said all this, I believe that in death we have another opportunity to decide the direction in which we now desire to move, towards purgation and sanctification, towards God or away from him. How often that opportunity will recur

---

[3] *Le Milieu Divin* (Collins 1960), p. 149.

I dare not say, only hope. I hold fast to Paul's confidence that God wills all men to be saved. I would like to believe that all men will be saved, but that can only happen with our consent. The choice is always ours.

In the nineteenth century the great incentive in the world mission of the Church was to save souls from hell-fire. Will the hope of universal salvation weaken the urgency of our appeal? Will it result in an indifference to moral values and ethical decisions? Or will the new emphasis be on the quality of life, the eternal life, the divine life which God wants all his created children to have, with a happy conviction that a day without Christ will be a wasted day, which we shall regret when we come to the light, and which will only immerse us more deeply in the futility and hopelessness of life until we do.

In my early years I listened to many sermons in Advent about what was called the four last things – death, judgment, hell and heaven. The first three subjects have their warnings, and the last holds out the hope of the promised land of eternity, where God's presence has all the positives which negate the first three: freedom, love, plenitude, holiness, the sharing of the divine nature; the fellowship with angels and saints and the spirits of just men made perfect; and the perfecting of relationships of love begun in this life and unbroken by the fact of death or that one partner in love has entered before the other into God's new order. It is good to meditate on 'the four last things', as long as we remember that there is a Fifth (though I hesitate in reverence and love to speak of him as a Fifth Thing) – God himself, the First and the Last, who planted his seed of eternity in each one of us, and wills and aids it to mature and grow until his personal creation of each is complete and perfect.

11

The Risen Life of Jesus

Jesus prepared his friends for his death, which he believed would be the only way of convincing people of his and God's unlimited love. He also assured them that their sense of his absence would be only for a short time: 'A little while and you will see me no more; and again a little while and you will see me' (John 16:16).

The 'little while' when they would not see him was barely more than thirty-six hours from just before sunset on Good Friday until just before dawn on the first day of the week. Those hours were a time of intense loss, desolation and mourning. But from that dawn onwards, one after another was to undergo a mystifying and quite unexpected experience of his presence.

Jesus encounters his disciples in different ways to teach them certain things: the women at the tomb are told that he is not there, the two on the Emmaus road now experience the fulfilment of the promise that when even two or three are together in his name, he is there; further, that when they break bread he is present. Peter is assured of forgiveness and continued authorization and commissioning; Thomas that he is still recognizable by spiritual nail-marks; the 120 are convinced of his guidance in filling up the place vacated by Judas; the 500 that no gathering is too large for him to teach; and the eleven in the Upper Room, still together, are given inspiration – the sharing of his spirit is seen already. When the disciples move up to Galilee he is found to be there already. They may have to face expulsion from the synagogue. When cross-examined by authorities they will be given a right and appropriate word; when stoned he will be there to enable them to endure; no fires in the arena or lions in the Coliseum will finally hurt them – like him they will cleanse evil infections, be defended against evil spirits, no bites from poisonous snakes will kill their true life. There will be angels to encourage and strengthen them, and no man-made gates shall be able to keep out their invasion of love and grace. The disciple will at last be as the Master (Luke 6:40).

It is interesting to note that in their experiences of the Risen Christ, there is some difficulty in recognizing him. Luke tells us that the two disciples on the way to Emmaus are sad, and that 'their eyes were kept from recognizing him' (Luke 24:16). As they sit down to the evening meal 'their eyes were opened and they recognized him; and he vanished out of their sight' (Luke 24:31). In a flash of vision and insight they realize that he has been with them on their walk, as well as in the blessing of God over the meal.

Mary at the tomb mistakes Jesus for the gardener. All that is in her mind is centred on the dead body and the renewal of the old relationship.

She is told that she must no longer keep him earthbound. A new era has dawned: Jesus is with the Father, yet in some mysterious way he is still with her and the men disciples (John 20:11–18).

The ten disciples behind bolted doors are suddenly aware that Jesus is present. He tells them that the mission to the world of which he has often spoken can now begin, for love has been shown to the uttermost, and forgiveness is available for all that has happened. They now have a gospel to preach. The Risen Lord present with them breathes into them his own spirit (John 20:19–23), and promises them that the moment to move outwards to the world will be shown to them and spiritual confidence and enablement supplied (Luke 24:49; Acts 1:3–4).

It is difficult for us to reconstruct a coherent timetable of all the experiences of the Risen Christ. His 'appearances' are unpredictable and unexpected. For example, Luke places the Ascending Christ in Bethany on the Mount of Olives, Matthew speaks of 'a mountain in Galilee to which Jesus had directed them' (Luke 24:50–3; Matthew 28:16–20). Luke speaks of the Ascending Lord as blessing his disciples: Matthew speaks of his promised presence with them until the end of time.

We earthbound creatures tend to think in our own dimensions of time and space and physical presence, which no longer apply to him. The resurrection would seem to be both a spiritual transformation and a transfiguration, to see which we need a new kind of sight. Our eyes have to be opened, our ears newly attuned to the divine voice

within, interpreting the past and pointing the way
for the future (Luke 24:25–7, 44–8).

The Risen Christ is no longer fixed in one or
successive localities. He is omnipresent, his
disciples will find him wherever they go, present in
everything that happens to them, simultaneously
present to every believer. The Jesus of the incarnate years, able to influence the situations in
which he is physically present, is now the cosmic
Christ, able to influence the totality of human life,
the divine plan for the fulness of time is now
operating (Ephesians 1:10; Colossians 2:9–10).

Paul speaks of the resurrection life as
completely essential to Christian faith. Without
that conviction our faith is futile and we are left
in our sins, all our loved ones who have died have
hopelessly perished, and we are of all people most
to be pitied (1 Corinthians 15:17–19). So he lists
the first witnesses: Peter, the twelve, more than
five hundred brethren, James the very down-to-
earth 'brother' of Jesus. Last of all he says that the
Risen Christ appeared to him. Every succeeding
disciple should be able to say this. The Risen
Christ comes to each of us: 'Behold, I stand at
the door and knock; if any one hears my voice
and opens the door, I will come in to him and eat
with him and he with me' (Revelation 3:20).

Paul might well have added the experience and
witness of Stephen, which had made such a deep
impression on him, though over months of stub-
born resistance he had kicked against the prick-
ings of conscience aroused by the memory. He
had probably been present at Stephen's trial,
when at the moment of violent accusation and

abuse Stephen had looked up to heaven and exclaimed, 'Behold, I see Jesus standing at the right hand of God'. An hour or two later Paul was certainly present at the stoning, for he heard him pray, 'Lord Jesus, receive my spirit', saw him kneel as the stones rained down upon him, and heard his loud cry, 'Lord, do not hold this sin against them' (Acts 7:56, 59, 60).

Later Peter would speak of the renewal of faith and hope brought about by the experience of disciples, not only in Jerusalem but in the dispersion of believers: 'Blessed be the God and Father of our Lord Jesus Christ! By his great mercy we have been born anew to a living hope through the resurrection of Jesus Christ from the dead' (1 Peter 1:3).

Another witness, whose experience, faith and hope not only endured but increased through a life of fifty or more years, is John. In his gospel the memories of his three years with the incarnate Christ seem to be interwoven with experiences of the Risen Christ. Many of the deepest crystallizations of faith seem not only shot through with memories but with deepening flashes of what Jesus means to him, as if he is saying, 'This is what Jesus says to me' about life and death, salvation and love, time and eternity, God and man. In his exile on Patmos John had plenty of time for reflection, meditation and communion with the Risen and Glorified Christ. In one particular vision he sees the Ascended Christ, 'his face like the sun shining in full strength', doubtless recalling his experience in the night of the transfiguration. Not only have his spiritual eyes been opened, but his spiritual hearing is awakened, and he hears a familiar voice: 'Fear not, I am the first and the last, and the living one; I died, and behold I am alive for evermore, and I have the keys of Death and Hades' (Revelation 1:17–18).

The experiences of Stephen and Paul, and the account given above of John, were all three outside the initial experiences related in the gospels, and so suggest that they were of the same character as spiritual experiences of people down the centuries, including people like ourselves living today. They may also give us some insight of what we may hope for and expect in the life of the world to come.

12

Blessings for Mourners

So far our attention has been focussed on the
dying and those we call dead. But for nearly
everyone who dies there are people who miss a
physical presence and grieve over their loss,
conscious perhaps of their own pain more than of
anxiety and uncertainty about the fate of the one
who has died. Sooner or later bereavement comes
to everyone, and often the greatest pain and sense
of loss come from the death of the one who is first
in our human affections and whom we value above
all others, perhaps a husband or wife with whom
we have had happy, loving, intimate relationship
through many years, or a much loved child, or a
loving parent or one whom we would call 'my
dearest friend'.

Jesus included among the blessings which follow
from living under the law of the Lord and being
faithful and grateful citizens of the kingdom of
heaven, a special beatitude for the bereaved:
'Blessed are those who mourn, for they shall be
comforted' (Matthew 5:4). He was promising us
a comfort and support far exceeding the most
overwhelming grief. St Paul in his Epistle to the
Romans speaks from both conviction and experi-

ence when he says: 'We know that in everything God works for good with those who love him, and are called according to his purpose' (Romans 8:28).

Two stiff conditions are attached to this promise: we must know God intimately and love him above even the dearest one; and we must try with heart, mind and will to live according to his will, believing it to be completely good, loving, right and effective, the best thing to be done in the worst of circumstances which are definitely not his will.

Paul ends this great chapter in Romans with an assurance which each of us must make his or her own: 'For I am sure that neither death, nor life, nor angels, nor principalities, nor things present, nor things to come, nor powers, nor height, nor depth, nor anything else in all creation, will be able to separate us from the love of God in Christ Jesus our Lord' (Romans 8:38–9).

There are two considerations which can save us from being knocked out by grief. The first is acceptance of the belief which is explicit in every book of the New Testament, that there is an after life and that the 'resurrection' of Jesus is not only evidence of this but also gives us some understanding of that risen life.

When John the Baptist in his loneliness and doubt sent messengers to Jesus, our Lord told those messengers: 'Go and tell John what you hear and see: the blind receive their sight and the lame walk, lepers are cleansed and the deaf hear, the dead are raised up, and the poor have good news preached to them' (Matthew 11:4–5).

Quite clearly Jesus did not on that occasion raise scores of dead people before the eyes of those present, but if he gave them the assurance that the physically dead are still spiritually living and his own certainty that the real person or self was not killed by physical death, that surely amounts to raising them from the dead.

St Paul comes to assure us again:

If we live, we live to the Lord, and if we die, we die to the Lord; so then, whether we live or whether we die, we are the Lord's. For to this end Christ died and lived again, that he might be Lord both of the dead and of the living. (Romans 14:8–9).

Because we belong to the God of life, who in his wisdom, love and hope created human life, he will not allow the life that he has given to be destroyed.

Yet grief that the dead are no longer in our physical sight is very understandable and necessary. My friend Helen Gold, to whom this book is dedicated, would have been a partner in its writing if she had not died of cancer. She had been a bereavement visitor for some years, and wrote to me several weeks before she died:

Grief is unique in every case, and falls into its own special category. I believe that grief has a task to fulfil which transcends the physical and emotional domain; that it can be an enemy but is meant to be a good friend. In other words, if allowed to be so, grief can be a great destroyer of all that is of value and significance in our personal life – but it can also be a great purifier and lifegiver. More precisely, I see grief as the natural emotional outlet, and in this function it belongs to our emotional make-up. It must be allowed to function and must not be suppressed. It must, however, not run wild for any great length of time but needs to be checked and eventually directed.

Further, it seems that grief is meant to be a gateway to our spiritual life. As such it can filter and purify the rubbish in thoughts, convictions, beliefs, attitudes and relationships which we have collected over the years, and which often act as barriers to the development of our spiritual life. Grief, in moments of its own peculiar lucidity, recognizes and discards that which is valueless and insincere in our particular life, and keeps the memory of that which is valuable. Consequently, the pain of grief can make us hard judges of ourselves and our actions, but at the same time can be a *redeemer* who dares us to leap over all that is past and have courage to start afresh; a *resurrector* who changes us into a new person, who uses past mistakes and sins as stepping-stones for a better life.

Anyone who has gone through bereavement, as well as friends who try to comfort and sustain them, will know of black moments of loneliness when we miss the physical sight of the one who has died, when we are reminded of the things we did together; or coming home from work or an absence to a smiling welcome; sitting together by the fireside reading or watching the television; stretching out a hand in the night just to touch the sleeping partner.

I remember a year or so ago going to visit the widow of a scholar whose books had been most helpful to me. She told me that although it was two years since he had died she wept every day for his loss. I found myself saying to her that possibly she was so submerged in her grief that she failed to be conscious of his spiritual presence with her. This was a new thought to her, and when some weeks later I called on her again she was a different woman and had asked her two grown-up children to drop in and add their gratitude to hers.

Another friend whose wife was dying of cancer was so stricken by that certainty that he could not restrain his prevenient grief and was making her grieve for him, mourning, as it were, before she died. Often other members of the family gathered round the sick bed are so sad that it must also sadden the dying, who is about to make the transition to a new and better life. Gratitude, love and hope should so fill our watching apprehensive hearts that we show our assurance that a relationship of love cannot be broken by physical death; each can assure the other that we shall keep in touch consciously every day and that we are both together in the new order which God has promised and provided.

Those who have been bereaved and those who regularly comfort and support them, tell us that to get adjusted to the death of a loved one may take as long as eighteen months or two years. It is a platitude to say that time is a great healer, and it is a failure in love to seek refuge in forget-fulness even for a day.

There are temptations in bereavement, especially in indulging in self-pity, rather than the willed continuance of love and the awareness and practice of presence. A friend who felt the death of his wife most keenly gradually became aware of these temptations. He writes:

Unless one has personally experienced the death of someone very close and dear, it is difficult to understand that there is a subtle and insidious element in bereavement which can deprive the bereaved of the chance of breaking old bonds and finding new and right attitudes (metanoia). Shock, desolation, pain, a sense of unreality, remorse, loneliness – these are all too familiar experiences for anyone who is bereaved. But with them also comes a wave of self-pity, which seems to last longer: and which is the hardest to overcome, because it contains within itself an element of satisfaction. For many months after the bereavement, one is an object of concern and compassion. Learning to live alone is a hard business: and friends are, naturally, sorry for you and do their best to help and comfort. One becomes a focus of sympathy: and that may be a novel experience – and not displeasing. Indeed, the bereavement is itself a dramatic experience, and the bereaved finds that he (or she) has a definite role to play in this drama. That role is enhanced by the feeling of unreality which bereavement brings. Even the desolation and the grief is partly relieved by the pictures one forms of oneself as the mourner, weeping over old photographs; seeing oneself as the tragic and lonely figure struggling to be brave, unconsciously soliciting the sympathy of friends over one's predicament. But self-pity, in any form, is wholly negative and destructive. The more that one is sorry for oneself, the less can one think positively about the person who had died.

It may take one or even two years before the stage of acceptance is reached. When it *is* reached – and the ties of the past are loosened, and the habitual ways of behaving and thinking are seen no longer to be appropriate – then there can come an abiding sense of peace and gratitude, and the wounds can be turned into blessings.

13

A Foolish Question?

In his great chapter on resurrection in the first letter to the Corinthians Paul says, 'But some man will say, How are the dead raised up? and with what body do they come?' (I Corinthians 15:35). He calls this a foolish question, but it is one that most of us ask, and one which people will continue to ask. It is natural that we should want to know what kind of a body we shall have after death, and what kind our ancestors and loved ones will have when we meet them again, as the New Testament assures us that we shall, in the new and eternal order of being.

As a choirboy in the early years of this century I used to sing a hymn[1] that pictured the rising from the grave of the physical body buried there to be united with the spirit from which it had been separated since death:

On the Resurrection morning
    Soul and body meet again.
No more sorrow, no more weeping
      No more pain.

[1] Hymns Ancient and Modern, no. 499.

The second verse of that hymn expected a long and welcome sleep:

> For a while the tired body
>   lies with feet towards the morn
> Till the last and brightest Easter
>   Day be born.

The third verse envisaged a reunion with loved ones:

> On that happy Easter morning,
>   All the graves their dead restore;
> Father, sister, child and mother
>   meet once more.

The resurrection is accepted as a fact: the end of pain, rest from the hardship of labour, ultimate reunion with loved ones. Human imagination went wrong about the 'how' of it.

In Advent time choir and congregation would sing:

> A few more years shall roll,
> A few more seasons come,
> And we shall be with those that rest
>   Asleep within the tomb.

We continued more realistically and hopefully:

> Then, O my Lord, prepare
> My soul for that great day,

O wash me in thy precious blood
  And take my sins away.[2]

Most people will have noticed that we are never conscious of how long we have been asleep, or indeed of the moment when we fall asleep. It may be that when we are asleep we are temporarily experiencing the different kind of time in God's new order.

Paul warns us that flesh and blood cannot inherit the kingdom of God. Could the 'body' be the entity in our total personality which gives form and animation to the flesh and blood? Indian friends speak of an astral body, which psychic people in the West claim to be able to see, a kind of aura which outlines what we speak of as the physical body.

The ordinary physical body is an amazing organism. Its growth from the union of a tiny egg and an equally tiny sperm excited the poet who wrote Psalm 139:13: 'I am fearfully and wonderfully made . . . and that my soul knoweth right well'. The seemingly exact dates at which certain organs are formed, the nine months pregnancy within the body of the mother until it is ready for the external world, the amazing processes of digestion, breathing, sewage, blood supply, the first smile and the first word and the first tottering steps, the gradual coordination of limbs, the healing properties seen in the covering of new skin over a graze or a cut or the setting of broken bones, and now the transplants, the exploits of

[2] ibid. no. 288.

athletes, the power of endurance, the expression of emotions, the power of reproduction and the union of bodies in sexual love, the yearning of man and wife for a child, parental and filial love enduring over scores of years, through misfortune, separation, and the consciousness that physical life will come to an end, and the hope of life beyond physical death – we can never exhaust the wonder of the miracle of life. An Australian poet, Bishop Gilbert White, called his body 'my dear lifelong comrade' and hoped that in some form it would survive death:

> 'Tis not thy fault thou canst no more obey
>   The eager spirit's bidding now grown slow,
>   Heavy and weighted with the load of years;
> How shall I greet thee that all wondrous day,
>   Endowed with tireless youth's immortal glow,
>   When God's calm face shall end my doubts
>   and fears?

Paul believed that God-in-Christ will change our present lowly body to be like his glorious body (Philippians 3:21). This 'perishable body', he says, 'must put on the imperishable, and this mortal nature must put on immortality' (1 Corinthians 15:53). Death is swallowed up in victory. At one time he, like most of us, regarded death as an enemy: 'The last enemy to be destroyed is death' (1 Corinthians 15:26); and he prays 'that I may know him and the power of his resurrection, and may share in his sufferings, becoming like him in his death, that if possible I may attain the resurrection from the dead' (Philippians 3:10–11). Only one Christian has gone further: Francis of Assisi praised God in his own Te Deum for our dear sister Death. Paul assures the Christians at Rome that the indwelling Spirit which raised Jesus from the dead is already at work within them to give life to their mortal bodies (Romans 8:11).

Our spirits, our real selves, express their feelings through our bodies – the look in the eyes, the smile or scowl in the face, the tone of voice, the warmth of the handshake, the eagerness or reluctance to help someone in need (not always what he says he needs, but his real need which may not be apparent to himself or the person he approaches). We recognize people by their bodies. So in the world of the spiritual we need a spiritual body, somehow the spiritualized successor to the physical one, with some recognizable features. Paul tells of his faith that God will give us a form or body appropriate to the new order.

My friend the Revd John Cole in a recent article wrote the following moving paragraphs:

The Archbishop of Canterbury, Dr Robert Runcie, tells how he once visited a hospice and there talked with a woman patient who was an artist and a potter, a creator of beautiful things, products of a soul able to perceive and to wonder. Before he left, she promised to send him the last thing she had made, the last she would ever make. In due course he received the gift, a piece of delicate pottery representing a broken and empty egg shell, a lasting testimony to her faith.

The broken, empty shell symbolized her broken and empty body, the chick that had emerged from it her soul, liberated into a fuller life than had been possible in the shell. . . .

With age there comes the sense, that with increasing bodily decrepitude, the soul has developed and matured in preparation for breaking out of the shell of the body into the life beyond.[3]

As a fellow priest who, in the last few years particularly, has like him been trusted by dying friends, I would add my grateful witness to his.

With this faith and examples of saintly lives all down the ages, we ought to be able to say in the moment of death and new life, as in every stage of life, 'Thou hast kept the good wine until now'.

The death of babies and young children presents a more painful problem. I have been very moved by parents who are told that the child they have been so eagerly expecting is stillborn, or will live only a few days: underneath the grief they seem glad that together they wanted to create new life. Even more moving is the often unexpressed desire of the mother to hold a stillborn child in her arms and give it a name; and the remark of a father whose child would not live long: 'We have to give a lifetime of love in a few days.' Fathers and mothers at such a time are evidence that men and women are indeed made in the image of God, the original, eternal, universal Parent, who has

---

[3] From 'A Glorious Flowering of the Soul' (*The Times,* 16 June 1984).

put into human nature a built-in quality of parent-
hood. A verse from another context can be
relevant here: 'Gather up the fragments that
nothing be lost'.

14

Crossing the Frontier

Not many people in robust health and not yet in advanced age-groups, are worried by thoughts of their own death. They may be saddened by the death of other people they loved, especially if they did not reach the average expectancy of life as calculated by life insurance experts: then they may wonder about life after death, and if there is any hope of keeping in touch. The very thought of life going on just as it is or has been may not be attractive. Here again our hopes and fears may be coloured by the words we use – 'everlasting' rather suggests mere survival, with life much as it has been; 'eternal' in its biblical sense speaks more of the quality of life. I find myself believing that everyone dying will survive, but in the moment after death they will be the same in character as the moment before death. I believe with deeper conviction and hope that those I love, and indeed everyone, will then have the opportunity of choice about the future, of decision about the direction in which they wish to move, or perhaps even an intention to remain earthbound and stagnant.

In any case I want to keep in touch, if there is any way of doing so. I recognize that I have to

earn a new way of consciousness and communication, which is now not dependent on physical
sight or audial sound or bodily presence, but on
a continuing relationship of love, in a milieu which
is God's creating, whose laws I am only just beginning to discover. I am living on the frontier
between this world's mode of being and communication and the next world's different mode. I have
previously moved across that frontier in prayer
and meditation, and now I can reinforce that
movement by the fact that over the border is a
loved one with whom I have been in closest intimate relationship for over fifty years, and who, I
know, is as eager to maintain that contact as I
am. She has experienced my state of being fully
and is now experiencing a different state. I, even
with the experience of quiet meditation, know
little of that new mode of being but am driven
by love and growing conviction to make more
determined and hopeful journeys across the frontier, and to be sensitive and expectant that my
life's partner will be doing the same, moving
towards me as I move towards her.

When my wife was with me in the present order
of being, we often talked of our intention to keep
in touch. We decided then that the onus of doing
this would rest on the one on the other side. I am
now more inclined to think that we were
mistaken. If the one who is 'left' (and I realise
more the difficulty of finding yet another right
word) does not really believe in the possibility of
continuing love, but keeps waiting for some
psychic happening to prove it, the unbroken link
that we both wanted then, and still do, will

weaken and possibly break altogether. So I accept
that the onus is on me, though I know in my
spiritual bones that she will be as eager to keep
in touch with me as I desire more than anything
else to keep in touch with her.

During one of my blackest periods of bereavement a fellow-sufferer referred me to Thomas
Hardy's poem, 'The Haunter', which he wrote in
the months following the death of his first wife.
It made me realise that I needed an extended
consciousness, a 'Brother Lawrence' type of practice of presence:

> He does not think that I haunt here nightly:
>   How shall I let him know
> That whither his fancy sets him wandering
>   I, too, alertly go? –
> Hover and hover a few feet from him
>   Just as I used to do,
> But cannot answer the words he lifts me –
>   Only listen thereto!
>
> When I could answer he did not say them:
>   When I could let him know
> How I would like to join in his journeys
>   Seldom he wished to go.
> Now that he goes and wants me with him
>   More than he used to do,
> Never he sees my faithful phantom
>   Though he speaks thereto.
>
> Yes, I companion him to places
>   Only dreamers know,
> Where the shy hares print long paces,
>   Where the night rooks go;

Into old aisles where the past is all to him,
  Close as his shade can do,
Always lacking the power to call to him,
  Near as I reach thereto!

What a good haunter I am, O tell him!
  Quickly make him know
If he but sigh since my loss befell him
  Straight to his side I go.
Tell him a faithful one is doing
  All that love can do,
Still that his path may be worth pursuing,
  And to bring peace thereto.

It would be a sad tragedy if my beloved felt
as unobserved as the imagined poet in Hardy's
haunting and very human lament.

Ladislaus Boros again comes to my comfort and
confirmation:

Every genuine lover affirms: 'It is impossible
for you not to be always with me. I myself,
loving you as I do, would no longer exist if you
no longer did. But I am alive and therefore so
are you, even if you are far from me, even
beyond the grave. I shall perhaps receive no
sign of your presence. But between us there
need be no sign and no verification. Nothing
that happens to us can destroy this eternity
inherent in our love. I should be consenting to
your destruction and my own, denying the very
nature of our love and, to the extent that it is
in my power, I should be handing you over to
eternal death, if I did not affirm with all the

force of my very existence as a person that you
will live on after death, whatever the superficial
evidence to the contrary.[1]

As Boros implies, no verification is needed or
demanded, but occasionally it is given. Two
experiences are gratefully in my memory. At the
cremation of my wife's body, I, with our three
children, was standing round the coffin just before
the words of committal when I felt her presence
beside me, looking young and smiling, pointing
towards the coffin and saying, 'That's not me!'
Nearly four years later a friend who had been
present told me that at the moment of committal
I turned and seemed to speak to someone who
was not visibly there.

The second experience followed about a fort-
night after the funeral, when I made the first
journey away from our home, to take part in a
day of meditation. I arrived the evening before at
the house where I was to spend the night. I was
shown into a room with a large window looking
out on to a lovely rock garden. Between myself
and the window, in an old fashioned chair very
similar to one of our own, it seemed that my wife
was sitting, smiling and saying, 'You see, I can
now come with you'. We had often been parted:
when we had a young family the cares of children
meant that I would have to go alone on pastoral
visits to the villages of the Irrawaddy Delta; once
we were parted for a whole year when she was
recuperating in England after an operation. In our

[1] *We are Future* (Search Press 1972), p. 71.

five years in Jerusalem half my time was spent in pastoral visits to English-speaking congregations in the Middle East or North Africa, and only occasionally was there enough money for both of us to go. But now I knew she could be with me wherever I went and whatever happened.

So I often call to her, and sometimes to other friends whom I knew and loved when we shared the same kind of human life. I do not often get worded intuitions, but sometimes when I wake in the night, as old people often do, I get a sense of warm presence, as if someone was sitting beside my bed, and I feel a caressing of the heart and fall happily asleep again. Those we call 'dead' may be out of physical sight, but never out of mind.

In meditation and intercession we move over the border into the country of the spirit. We are accustomed to think that when we pray for others we are linking ourselves with their need on the one hand and with God's abounding grace on the other. Sometimes, however, I get the strong feeling that in intercession God links us with those for whom we are concerned, whether they be physically with us in this order of being or in God's new order.

I also find that I understand my wife better now than I did when we were both in this present order. Things that used to puzzle me now seem clear. Sometimes I find myself saying, 'If I had only known then what I know now, I could have been more understanding and loving.'

On the night my wife 'died', unable to sleep, I read again a favourite poem written by Elizabeth Barrett Browning:

How do I love thee? Let me count the ways.
I love thee to the depth and breadth and height
My soul can reach, when feeling out of sight
For the ends of Being and ideal Grace.
I love thee to the level of every day's
Most quiet need, by sun and candle light.
I love thee freely, as men strive for Right;
I love thee purely, as they turn from Praise.
I love thee with the passion put to use
In my old griefs, and with my childhood's faith.
I love thee with a love I seemed to lose
With my lost saints – I love thee with the
      breadth,
Smiles, tears, of all my life! – and, if God
      choose,
I shall but love thee better after death.[2]

When my father-in-law was dying of cancer
thirty years ago, my wife used to sit with him
whenever she could, and they would talk together
of the old friends he would soon meet, particularly
his Irish forbears, and some of his employers with
whom he had been great friends. Once a week I
go back through a now very long list of relatives,
friends, teachers and benefactors, grateful
thoughts mingling with stirrings of conscience that
I had not been more explicit in my gratitude and
less critical of what seemed to be their blemishes.

It may be that when we are striving to live in
the spirit of the Kingdom, time loses the sense of
duration and acquires a feeling of simultaneous-
ness. If that is so, it may be possible to go back

[2] From *Sonnets from the Portuguese*.

into the past (as we would speak of it) and forgive
and be forgiven, somehow to heal the hurts of the
past. If that is so with us on this side of the frontier, it must be more so with those on the other
side.

I have sometimes been called to comfort the
family of someone who has 'committed suicide',
when relatives have realized that they might have
been more helpful, loving and sympathetic to one
who lived in deep depression or in despairing
remorse. God's reconciliation must be eternal, his
forgiveness unlimited, though perhaps that
forgiveness, given before we repent, can only
operate when we accept it, that is when we repent.
So we may comfort one another, in whatever state
of being they may be, by the comfort with which
we ourselves are comforted by God (2 Corinthians
1:4).

Very often I find that dying people feel the
nearness of dead loved ones, as in the Negro spiritual 'Swing low, sweet chariot . . . a band of
angels coming after me, coming for to carry me
home'. We can hope and believe that our dearest
ones are allowed to know how we are faring and
will be at hand to welcome us when we die, to
show us round the spiritual mansions of our
Father's house, and introduce us to loved ones
earlier arrived, and perhaps new acquaintances
whom they have got to know.

Let me close this rambling in the frontier
countryside of the human spirit, the home which
God has prepared for all, if all will accept it, by
remembering a very recent in-seeing. A few weeks
ago I was introduced to a flower-seller in

Lausanne, who told me of a lovely and much-loved little daughter who had 'died' a few months earlier. The mother said that the child had had absolutely no fear of dying and a few days before it happened had said, 'Mummy, whenever you are in any trouble, just tell me and I'll tell Jesus, and he will take care of you'. That little one had already crossed the frontier – both ways!

15

Our Risen Life

Jesus promised his first disciples that when they
were fully taught they would be like their teacher
(Luke 6:40), and that because he lives, they would
live also (John 14:19). We can therefore get some
idea of our own possible life after death, by
looking at his risen life. He was now no longer
under the limitations of time, space and physical
body. He did not have to take two hours in
walking from the two disciples at the supper table
in Emmaus to the ten disciples in the Upper Room
in Jerusalem. He could move at will in an almost
immediacy of time. No barred doors could keep
him out. In the garden of the tomb, Mary Magda-
lene experiences him warning her not to imprison
him in the past or cling to his physical body, for
he is in God's new order of being, he is with God
in an altogether new way. Wherever God is, he
will now be, not localized in one place, but omnipresent everywhere and always. John Hick says,
'The result of this is that the Christ-Spirit,
restricted during the period of the incarnation to
exerting an influence in one place at a time, is
now able to influence the world as a whole,
changing the environment in which men have ever

since lived.'[1] And John Hick who has studied the insights of Karl Rahner very closely, also says:

> Rahner suggests that the soul which in this life is exclusively related to one particular bit of the world, namely a human body, is at death released from that limitation and becomes related to the world as a whole . . . it becomes detached from matter, totally out of this world and no longer related to the space-time continuum.[2]

It is almost unbelievable that the physical world should be open to the soul in the after life, that it may so be to any other soul, still in this incarnation, in a moment of time. I can only say that I, for one, need a lot more purifying, sanctifying, perfecting, to enable me to think it possible, and in grateful faith practise it.

In the ordinary course of human life it will not be many more years before I make the transition to the world of eternity and spirituality. If there is memory, and I have said already that I believe there will be, I hope that I may remember this tremendous hope, and submit to God's cleansing but not destructive fire, so that forgiven and purified I may receive his gift, and be allowed to cooperate in his plan of world sanctification and salvation, from that new order of being.

Each one of us will need a new kind of spiritual

[1] *Death and Eternal Life* (Collins 1976), p 240.
[2] ibid., p. 228; see also Karl Rahner, *On the Theology of Death*. Search Press 1969.

sight and hearing, we shall need to be partakers of the divine nature (2 Peter 1:4), we shall need a love of all our human siblings, as John saw in his first epistle: 'We know that we have passed out of death into life, because we love the brethren' (1 John 3:14). If we are to qualify for the new being which God has planned, it will only be through the gift of love, which is God himself, the Source of all love.

The writer of the Epistle to the Hebrews speaks encouragingly of the end of the pilgrimage of the human soul as being the spiritual Mount Zion, 'the city of the living God, the heavenly Jerusalem, and to innumerable angels in festal gathering, and to the assembly of the first-born who are enrolled in heaven, and to a judge who is God of all, and to the spirits of just men made perfect, and to Jesus . . .' (Hebrews 12:22–4).

So far I have only spoken of the hope of sharing Christ's risen life, in the new order beyond death. May it not be possible to have a foretaste, a first instalment while still in the present order of being? Father Harry Williams suggests that it is:

> To be raised from the dead is to be no longer the prisoner of one's environment. It is to be free from the chains of one's conditioning. It is to realize that it is not necessary to play the game which is being played on us, so that we can play our own game not the one imposed.[3]

And George Macdonald, the Scottish minister

[3] H. Williams, *True Resurrection*. Fount 1983.

whom C. S. Lewis in his anthology of quotations speaks of as posthumously responsible for his conversion, adds his tribute and insight:

> When a man is true, if he were in hell he could not be miserable. He is right with himself because right with Him whence he came. To be right with God is to be right with the universe: one with the power, the love, the will of the mighty Father, the cherisher of joy, the Lord of laughter, whose are all glories, all hopes, who loves everything and hates nothing but selfishness.[4]

Paul speaks of being risen with Christ even now, but implies that to be risen with him we must also have died with him: 'I have been crucified with Christ; it is no longer I who live, but Christ who lives in me; and the life I now live in the flesh I live by faith in the Son of God, who loved me and gave himself for me' (Galatians 2:20).

Paul was often in danger of physical death, but he was always conscious of the imperative to die to sinfulness, selfishness, self-will and lovelessness. 'I die every day', he says to his friends at Corinth (1 Corinthians 15:31), a text which says to me that I have to repudiate my lower nature and egoistic tendencies, if I am to live the risen life now. I have to give God priority in everything as Jesus did, love him above everything else and everyone else. So I pray:

---

[4] C. S. Lewis, *George Macdonald: an anthology*. Fount 1983.

O God, I know that if I do not love You with all my heart, mind and will, I shall love something else with all my heart, mind and will. Grant that putting You first in all my loving I may be liberated from all lesser loves and loyalties, and have You as my first love, my chiefest good, my greatest joy. I know, dear Father, if I do love You in this way, all other loves and dearest human loves fall into place and are deepened and enhanced.

Not only must I model my life on the human life of Jesus, as portrayed so convincingly in the gospels, I must have his mind and attitude to others, seeing in each the seed of deification, often hardly germinating or stunted in growth, but often also seen flowering in simple, humble, loving souls. To help me in that divine and human imitation, I can and must be open to his risen life, which will inspire me, strengthen me, show me how in this amazing yet difficult modern world, he is interpretative, relevant and contemporary.

In faithfulness to him and to our common Father, there can be a new understanding of death, now accepted not as an enemy but as a friend. There will come a compassion and care for the bereaved, not only in the first news of their 'loss' and at the funeral of the vacated shell, but in the weeks and months of apparent loneliness. Here we must be practical – a regular visit, a frequent telephone call, an invitation to a meal, not shrinking from mentioning quite happily the risen one's name, recalling happy memories, eager to see that the people and things he cared

for most in his lifetime continue to be cared for,
conscious that he or she is still present in a new
order of being.

So death is no longer to be feared, especially
when it comes after a long and fulfilled life. If
it comes prematurely through war, disease, the
assassin's bullet, or starvation, it arouses more
grief, yet even then we can trust the God and·
Father of Jesus Christ to see that his loving
purpose is not frustrated, trusting his neighbour
children to comfort those in any trouble by the
comfort with which we ourselves are comforted
by God. Directly or indirectly the comfort comes
from him.

Paul learnt from the Risen Christ as much as
from those who had seen him physically that

> though our outer nature is wasting away, our
> inner nature is being renewed every day. For
> this slight momentary affliction is preparing for
> us an eternal weight of glory beyond all
> comparison, because we look not to the things
> that are seen but the things that are unseen; for
> the things that are seen are transient, but the
> things that are unseen are eternal! So we do not
> lose heart. (2 Corinthians 4:16–18)

Almost his last words to his beloved son in faith
Timothy become relevant to us also: 'The Lord
will rescue me from every evil and save me for
his heavenly Kingdom. To him be the glory for
ever and ever. Amen' (2 Timothy 4:18).

In fact when death comes in God's way it is to
be welcomed. It is for all of us eventually the end

of ageing, dying and pain. Keeping in touch with the Creator we are kept young in spirit, we can continue the maturation and sanctification already begun by God, we can keep in touch with the beautiful things of this world and the loved ones still here, and enjoy once again the *full* relationship with loved ones there already. Both New Testament and Old tell us of the great joys ahead, 'Eye has not seen, nor ear heard, neither have entered into the heart of man, the things which God has prepared for them that love him' (1 Corinthians 2:9; Isaiah 64:4).

And we may add, 'and also for them that do not yet love him', for when they see him as he really is, revealed and embodied in Jesus Christ, his life, death and heavenly life, they will feel that they have at last come home, however far they may have strayed, to a home they have always longed for, and where the Eternal Father stands with outstretched arms!

V.   This is the gospel of death.
R.   Thanks be to You, O God, for this your glorious gospel.

16

Prayers for Two Worlds

A prayer for all times

O Lord Jesu Christ, who hast made me and redeemed me and brought me where I am upon my way: Thou knowest what thou wouldst do with me; do with me according to thy will, for thy tender mercies' sake.

King Henry VI (1421–71)

Hearts to Heaven

Grant, we beseech thee, Almighty God, that like as we do believe thy only-begotten Son our Lord Jesus Christ to have been exalted by Thee into the heavens; so we may also in heart and mind thither ascend, and with him continually dwell, who liveth and reigneth with Thee and the Holy Ghost, one God, world without end. Amen.

Collect for Ascension Day,
Book of Common Prayer

Make us conscious of your presence, O God,
And of our Saviour Christ ever present with
You

in the centre of power,
in the origin of love,
in the source of saving activity,
confident in your will
that our human nature shall be
sanctified and perfected
gathered into the divine love
and blessed to all eternity.

G.A.

Everpresent

Abide with us, O Lord, for it is toward evening
and the day is far spent: abide with us, and with
thy whole Church. Abide with us in the evening
of the day, in the evening of life, in the evening
of the world. Abide with us and with all thy
faithful ones, O Lord, in time and in eternity.

Lutheran Manual of Prayer

Time and Eternity

O God, the protector of all that trust in thee,
without whom nothing is strong, nothing is holy;
increase and multiply upon us thy mercy; that,
thou being our ruler and guide, we may so pass
through things temporal, that we lose not the
things eternal: grant this, O heavenly Father, for
Jesus Christ's sake our Lord.

Book of Common Prayer

O Lord God of time and eternity, who makest us creatures of time that, when time is over, we may attain thy blessed eternity: with time, thy gift, give us also wisdom to redeem the time, lest our day of grace be lost; for our Lord Jesus' sake.

Christina Georgina Rossetti (1830–84)

God of eternity, whose blessed Son lived in time to show us the divine and eternal life, so that we serving Thee in time might learn something of thy divine life and even now begin to experience the timelessness of heaven. Grant that being made in your image, time may merge into eternity, the material into the spiritual, the mortal into the immortal, faith into sight, so that I may grow into the spiritual stature and character of your perfect Son and be finished and complete as You intended me to be at my spiritual birth.

G.A.

O Creator God, my body is growing old and weak, my memory is failing. Keep me young in spirit, help me to believe that I am being hollowed out of the physical, material and temporal, so that I may be filled with the spiritual and eternal. Let me not fear the death of the body, but know that it is the transition to your eternal order of being, of which I see glimpses as I study the risen life of your blessed Son and through him keep in close touch with You, the Source of both life and love, blessed for ever.

G.A.

Death

O God, we thy creatures try to evade the fact of death, and to keep it out of mind, yet in our deeper moments we know it is a warning note, urging us so to die every day to all selfishness and sin, that when the time comes for our final migration, we may take death in our stride because life is so strong within us, as it was in him who was so manifestly thy true Son and so convincingly the prototype of thy finished humanity, even Jesus Christ, thy Son, our brother.

G.A.

We are all mortal, O Lord,
and our future lies with Thee.
Make us so conscious of Thee that death may
   be
no break but a new dimension of being,
better than anything so far.
Help us to leave no duty undone,
no sin unrepented,
no relationship unsanctified,
and grant us the faith that the best is yet to
   be.
So let us live in hope and love
and joyful expectation,
Without fear and without regret,
knowing Thee to be the God and Father of
Jesus Christ, and our Father, and
the God and Father of all.

G.A.

O Lord Christ, you spoke of the time when the dead would hear your voice, calling them by name and promising that all who answered would live: the little girl only a few minutes dead, heard you call 'Little one' and felt your gentle touch; the young man a few hours dead, his corpse on the way to the grave heard your command and was restored to his heartbroken mother; Lazarus in the tomb four days heard your loud shout and hobbled forth in the grave clothes. So you taught us that in every kind of death, at every stage in it, you are there to call each by name and give something better than physical life. Dear Lord, my loved ones are safe with you, and I shall be safe. I lift my heart to you and the Father in grateful thanks for them and for myself, O ever-living, everloving, never-failing Lord.

G.A.

For the dying

O holy and eternal Lord,
You know and we know
how much the souls of the dying
need your forgiveness and sanctifying
before they feel at home in your presence.
Grant that in the clear light of eternity
we all may see our need,
and accept the grace and love
which you have ever offered us
since the moment of our creation.
So most gracious God, You will be to us

our Redeemer as well as our Creator,
as shown us through Jesus Christ, our Lord.

G.A.

Into they merciful hands, O Lord, we commend
the soul of this thy servant, now departing from
the body. Acknowledge, we meekly beseech
Thee, a work of thine own hands, a sheep of thine
own fold, a lamb of thine own flock, a sinner of
thine own redeeming. Receive him into the
blessed arms of thine unspeakable mercy, into
the sacred rest of everlasting peace, and into the
glorious estate of thy chosen saints in heaven.

Bishop Cosin (1160–74)

For all who mourn

O merciful Lord God, who has given us thy Son
to be the bright and morning star, and to give
light to them that sit in darkness and in the shadow
of death: look, we pray Thee, upon all whose
hearts are troubled by the loss of those whom they
love; draw them beneath the shadow of thy wings;
enlighten their eyes that they may endure as
seeing the invisible; and cheer them with largeness
of hope and confidence in thy eternal purpose;
through Jesus Christ our Lord.

J. Armitage Robinson (1911–33)

Lord, all these years we were so close to one
another, we did everything together, we seemed
to know what each was feeling, without the need

of words, and now she is gone. Every memory hurts . . . sometimes there comes a feeling that she is near, just out of sight. Sometimes I feel your reproach that to be so submerged in grief is not to notice that she is eager to keep in touch with me, as I with her. O dear Lord, I pray out of a sore heart that it may be so, daring to believe that it can be so.

G.A.

For the risen ones

O Father of all, we pray to Thee for those whom we love but see no longer. Grant them thy peace; let light perpetual shine upon them; and in thy loving wisdom and almighty power work in them the good purpose of thy perfect will; through Jesus Christ our Lord.

Book of Common Prayer 1928

Almighty God, whose love is over all thy works in this and every world; into thy hands we commit the souls of those whom Thou hast taken into the world of light, beseeching Thee to grant unto them the unutterable joys of thine eternal kingdom, and unto all who mourn them grace to abide thy will in fortitude of spirit and in perfect faith.

Anon.

We give back to You, O God, those whom You gave to us. You did not lose them when You gave them to us, and we do not lose them by their return to You. Your dear Son has taught us that life is eternal and love cannot die. So death is only a horizon, and a horizon is only the limit of our sight. Open our eyes to see more clearly, and draw us closer to You, that we may know that we are nearer to our loved ones who are with You. You have told us that You are preparing a place for us: prepare us also for that happy place, that where You are we may also be always, O dear Lord of life and death.

William Penn

At the grave

Grant, O Lord, that as we are baptized into the death of thy blessed Son our Saviour Jesus Christ, so by continual mortifying our corrupt affections we may be buried with him; and that through the grave, and gate of death, we may pass to our joyful resurrection; for his merits, who died, and was buried, and rose again for us, thy son Jesus Christ our Lord.

Book of Common Prayer

O Creator Father, we have come to dispose reverently of the outworn body of this our loved one, believing that (s)he has been born into the sphere of the eternal and spiritual which touches this sphere of time and matter in which we all begin and from which we must all one day move: increase our faith in thy unfailing love from which

nothing in life or death can separate us: through
him who himself lived our life, died and was
buried and was raised by Thee to endless life, who
spans this world and the next, matter and spirit,
time and eternity, and is Lord of life and death,
gathering all willing souls into eternal life, even
Jesus Christ, thy beloved Son and our dear Lord
and Brother, blessing and blessed for evermore.

G.A.

Thanks for loved ones

O Lord our God, from Whom neither life nor
death can separate those who trust in thy love,
and whose love holds in its embrace thy children
in this world and in the next: so unite us to thyself
that in fellowship with Thee we may be always
united to our loved ones whether here or there;
give us courage, constancy, and hope; through
Him who died and was buried and rose again for
us, Jesus Christ our Lord.

William Temple (1881–1944)

O God, our Father, we thank Thee for the love
and blessing that has come into our lives through
these our loved ones who are now hidden from
our physical sight. We know that they are still
living in Your world of spirit. Grant them the
assurance of Your continuing presence and love.
Cleanse them from all weakness and sin. Help
them to grow to that ideal which is thy plan for
them. Warm their hearts with the love of our

prayers and keep their memory strong and fresh
in our minds, that we may meet them still with
loving and joyful hearts, grateful to Thee through
our Lord Jesus Christ.

G.A.

O dear Lord, I am learning to trust You
   not for myself alone
but for those also whom I love
and who seem hidden
by the shadow death;
that, as I know your power to have raised
our Lord Jesus Christ from the dead,
so I may trust your love
to give eternal life
to all who believe in him;
through the same Jesus Christ our Lord.

G.A.

Judgment

Withhold not from me, O my God, the best, the
Spirit of thy dear Son; that in that day when the
judgment is set I may be presented unto Thee not
blameless, but forgiven, not effectual but faithful,
not holy but persevering, without desert but
accepted, because he hath pleaded the causes of
my soul, and redeemed my life.

Eric Milner-White (1884–1963)

O Master, taught by you I know that my daily
sleep is like a little death: as it comes may I

undergo a little judgment of the past day, so that every wrong deed and unholy thought may be recognized and confessed, then nothing will go down into the depths of my being which has not been forgiven and sanctified. Then I shall be ready for my final judgment and look forward with hope and love to standing before You, holy judge and loving Saviour.

G.A.

Looking back

Lord, looking back on my journey so far, I see how your love and goodness have been with me, through many failings and dangers, in many joys and adventures. I have received much love from friends, enjoyed so many good and lovely things, been guided and inspired by the wisdom and encouragement of many teachers and writers. Often I have felt your presence near, and sometimes I have had to walk by faith.

Forgive my slowness, my failures in faith, the smallness of my love, my poor use of your grace.

Accept my heart's thanks for growing knowledge of You, for increasing assurance of your purpose of love and deepening knowledge of the things that are eternal. As I turn again to the journey ahead, it is bright with the remembrance of past mercies, dear Father and Saviour.

G.A.

There will come a time when my links with earth

will grow weaker, when my powers fail, when I must bid farewell to dear ones still rooted in this life with their tasks to fulfil and their loved ones to care for, when I must detach myself from the loveliest things and begin the lonely journey. Then I shall hear the voice of my beloved Christ saying 'It is I, be not afraid'. So with my hand in his, from the dark valley I shall see the shining City of God and climb with quiet and trusting steps and be met by the Father of souls and clasped in the everlasting arms.

G.A.

Life's offering

On the day when death will knock at my door what shall I offer Thee, either in the closing minutes of this life or in the opening minutes of my new birth in the life beyond? Oh, I will set before Thee all the lovely things that I have seen, all the love that I have received and given, all the insights of truth that I have gathered, all the things that I have valued and enjoyed, all the tasks completed or left for others, all my gratitude and love for the past, all my enjoyment of the present and my hope for the future. Above all I will offer my recognition that You are with me in the moment of death, as You have been in every moment of my mortal life. So You will lead me into the new order You in your goodness have prepared for me.

Inspired by Rabindranath Tagore

Heaven or hell

> O my God,
> if I worship Thee in desire for heaven,
>   exclude me from heaven;
> if I worship Thee for fear of hell,
>   burn me in hell.
> But if I worship Thee for thyself alone,
> then withhold not from me thine eternal
>   beauty.

Rabi'a (*c.* A.D. 800)

O Lord God, I thank You for the insight You have put into my heart that hell is not your intention or creation, but that we make our own hells. I thank You even more gratefully for the releasing word that the door is never locked but that at any moment I may come forth into the freedom and light of heaven, so gloriously your eternal creation, open to all.

G.A.

> Heaven is, dear Lord, where'er Thou art,
> O never then from me depart;
> For to my soul 'tis hell to be
> But for one moment void of Thee.

Bishop Ken (1637–1711)

O God, who hast prepared for them that love Thee such good things as pass man's understanding: Pour into our hearts such love toward Thee, that we, loving Thee above all things, may

obtain thy promises, which exceed all that we can
desire; through Jesus Christ our Lord.

Book of Common Prayer

The God of peace,
   that brought again from the dead
      our Lord Jesus,
   that great shepherd of the sheep
      through the blood of the
      everlasting covenant,
   make us perfect in every good work
      to do his will,
   working in us that which is
   well-pleasing in his sight;
      through Jesus Christ,
   to whom be glory for ever and ever.

Hebrews 13:2–21 (A.V.)